# A PANORAMA OF GAFF RIG

by

JOHN LEATHER

Illustrated by
ROGER SMITH

BARRIE & JENKINS
COMMUNICA - EUROPA

First published in 1977 by
Barrie & Jenkins Limited
24 Highbury Crescent, London N5 1RX


Copyright © John Leather 1977


ISBN 0 214 20393 X

Printed by Ebenezer Baylis & Son Ltd
The Trinity Press, Worcester, and London

Designed by John Leath

# LIST OF ILLUSTRATIONS

# INTRODUCTION

Gaff rig is resurgent in the sailing world of Britain, Europe, Scandinavia, North America and the Antipodes. Old craft are being re-fitted with half-forgotten sails, rigging and gear, and more important, new hulls are being designed, built and rigged, often as replicas or in imitation of traditional working craft, and sometimes as new concepts using the best of seaworthy yacht practice, with the efficiency of the gaff rig enhanced by the use of modern materials of great strength, for masts, spars, sails and rigging.

This panorama is not intended as a comprehensive study but as a selective glimpse into the past and present sailing of gaff-rigged yachts and other craft. It illustrates through the splendid photographs from Roger M. Smith's collection and the comments on them, a variety of type and size of craft which have used the rig and something of the life and atmosphere on board them; the speed of some and the stubborn seafaring which was the lot of others. Until only 60 years ago, gaff rig predominated in the British, North American, European and Scandinavian sailing world, for work or pleasure, and attained a particularly high standard of efficiency in fishing vessels and yachts. Much of its history has been expressed definitively in the author's book *Gaff Rig*.

It is still interesting to imagine what it was like to race in a large gaff cutter, sharing with perhaps 30 other hands, a captain and two mates, the thrill of putting 14,000 square feet of canvas on one mast to windward in a breeze, with the added majesty of her 10,000 square feet spinnaker when running. Such seamanship was learned in humbler vessels; small fishing smacks and coasting craft, designed, built and owned by men used to a hard school of endeavour, where windward ability often meant the difference between saving or missing the tide, between profit and loss, and sometimes between life and death.

Gaff rig continued to be used and to develop in cargo and fishing vessels until about 1910, then it declined, though gaff sailed craft of these categories continued in use until the 1940s and were occasionally still built during the interval, usually with auxiliary engines of increasing power.

During the 20th century yachtsmen have gradually become the sailors of the sail. Gaff and lugsail rigs dominated the sport until the emergence of numbers of Bermudan rigged racing and cruising yachts during the 1920s, after designers of small racing yachts re-discovered the windward ability of the tall triangular sail which had appeared in isolated British yachts during the 19th century, and was used in many fishing and cargo craft from Bermuda, the West Indies and the Chesapeake Bay region of America.

While the smaller racing classes were being built or re-rigged with Bermudan sails in an uncompromising quest for windward efficiency, gaff sails lingered in the British first-class racing yachts until 1930, challenged by new Bermudan rigged competitors. The large gaff rigged racers tried hard to keep up with 'Marconi' top masts rearing ever higher until, by the mid 1920s, the rigs were as extreme in height and staying, and as vulnerable in strong winds as any of the later 'J' class racers, with which nowadays they are often confused; many suffering similar loss of masts and withdrawal from races from this excess.

As racers adopted Bermudan rig during the 1920s and became widespread by the early 1930s, gaff rig increasingly became identified with cruising yachts, but the influence of offshore racing, then generally encouraging a healthy type of yacht, gradually swept away much prejudice against Bermudan rig in yachts for rigorous sea and ocean use, until gaff sails came to be associated with a 'husky cruiser' tradition, evinced by the refitting and conversion of smacks, pilot cutters and other ex-working craft, and yachts inspired by these types. Cruising men split between protagonists of Bermudan or gaff rig; a division lasting into the 1940s and which caused more argument than even the Americas Cup Races.

After 1945 the sailing world generally had little use for gaff sails for many years, though occasional examples were designed and built and many existing boats retained the rig in Britain.

A revival commenced during the late 1950s and gathered momentum during the following decade to become re-established as a vigorous part of the sailing scene It has grown and spread abroad from England during recent years, and shows no sign of slackening.

There are many aspects of this revival of interest in a rig used in a wide variety of hull forms. It is more subtle than just a reaction to the now widespread use of the triangular Bermudan rig in yachts. To some it offers the opportunity to prove they can sail like their forefathers did, to others it gives the pleasure of restoration of an old craft to her former appearance and rig, and the subsequent pleasures and worries of handling under sail. Many have been attracted to the rig during the past 15 years.

I was exposed to gaff rig at an early age as my grandfather and his forefathers had for generations owned cutter and ketch rigged fishing smacks, sailing from the Essex village of Rowhedge, on the river Colne. In summer, relatives were captains of many gaff rigged and other yachts, large and not so large, racers and cruisers. My grandmother's family, the Cranfields, of the same village of yachtsmen and fishermen, were also a noted family of racing yacht captains and smack owners, two of whom three times captained challengers for the Americas Cup, the largest racing yachts of history.

When I graduated from sailing small open boats as a shipbuilding apprentice in the 1940s, I built myself a 24 ft gaff cutter, and soon after began designing gaff rigged craft; a practice which my yacht racing relatives regarded as a severe step backwards from the proved windward efficiency of Bermudan rig! However, they and many others then living in our part of seafaring Essex, were kind enough to take interest in my efforts, and I learned much from their experienced comment as well as from the ownership of several Bermudan rigged craft, which provided a comparison of ability and handling characteristics.

Work on the design and construction of modern commercial craft, particularly of small fishing and coasting vessels and yachts of all types, also gave me an insight into the ingenuity and skill of earlier designers and builders and increased my admiration for the skill, fortitude and energy of those who worked under sail in small fore and aft rigged craft.

The photographs range from 1890 to the present, and have been chosen to express some trend of type, notability, or interesting features of hull and rig.

The older photographs, which are from the historical collection of Roger N. Smith, were taken on 12 in × 10 in glass plates, each weighing about 1 lb in its wooden plate holder, with a large, wooden camera weighing 10–15 lb, so the photographer's equipment for a day's shooting of perhaps 20 exposures might weigh about 35 lb. Having chosen the yacht or incident he wished to photograph from the slow steam launch or rowing boat used for his work, he had to analyse accurately, the distance and angle so that he and the yacht arrived at the desired position at the right moment. The depth of focus of such large cameras was very narrow because of the large format used and this further restricted a photographer's scope. Changing slides took about 2 minutes before another picture could be taken. A realisation of these difficulties increases our admiration for the high quality of the results. The negatives were processed for either contact printing on gaslight paper or enlargement through a daylight enlarger, often fitted in the roof of the photographer's premises to obtain north light. If the plates were not washed sufficiently the silver remained active and resulted in deterioration of the image. Glass negatives are also easily cracked and chipped but many remain sound as a fascinating record of a vanished era in sailing.

The more recent photographs are by Roger M. Smith. He specialised in colour photography for pictorial uses, besides black and white, and established his business as a marine and general photographer at Cowes in the early 1960s. In contrast to the old timers, he works with a roll-film camera producing 6 × 7 cm negatives with 10 exposures to a roll and weighing about 2 lb. He uses several cameras with lenses of differing focal lengths. Most photographs are taken in colour, which can be readily produced in black and white if desired, as in this book. He uses a rigid bottom inflatable boat with a 50 h.p. outboard motor, capable of about 28 knots and of being used at sea in rough conditions. It can be towed on a trailer to launch in many places around the coast, enabling him to cover many marine events and subjects.

It is hoped the book will serve as a reminder of the variety of the gaff rig in arrangement and methods of rigging, the types of craft it propelled and, not least, the men who used it for work or pleasure.

## 1  Satanita

The 300 ton yawl *Satanita* winning the Queen's Cup in a strong wind, 1900. This famous racer was the fastest reaching yacht built when new and cutter rigged, averaging 13.7 knots during a race from Gravesend around the Mouse light vessel and back, on a broad and a close reach.

Her dimensions were 131 ft 6 in overall, 93 ft 6 in waterline, 24 ft 6 in beam and 14 ft 6 in draught. She displaced 126 tons and sail area was 10,094 square feet, of which 5246 was in the mainsail.

*Satanita* was designed by Joseph Soper, who received the commission on Christmas Day 1892. He worked all through the holidays and long after, to produce his masterpiece, which was built by J. G. Fay and Co. Ltd. at Southampton for A. D. Clark and was launched in the spring of 1893, to be raced by captain Thomas Jay of Rowhedge, Essex, with a crew from that small Essex village of racing skippers and hands which that year provided the captains and crews for three of the four new big racers: Captain John Carter in the royal cutter *Britannia* and Captain William Cranfield in the *Valkyrie II*. Command of the similar Scottish cutter *Calluna* was also offered to Captain Carter, who decided in favour of the royal cutter. It was a rare compliment to a community of 1000 people.

In 1898 the *Satanita* was altered to a yawl rig of 10,300 square feet and when this photograph was taken she was under the gold star flag of Sir Maurice Fitzgerald and was sailed by Captain Diaper of Itchen, Hampshire.

Here, 13 hands and a couple of guests are getting the staysail sheet home on the lee side. The first mate stands by the mast. The second mate is assisting the captain at the tiller lines. The mainsheet man stands ready by the fall and other hands are alert about the deck.

Although there is little noticeable sea, it was blowing hard when this photograph was taken as the topmast is housed and the jib-headed mizzen set in place of the gaff sail, which has been unbent and stowed below before the start. She is hard on the wind and the gaff is bending under the thrust of the unreefed mainsail. The mastheadsmen are aloft, checking the throat halyard. The easy grace of the outreaching bow and long counter suggest speed. The streaming deck contrasts with the open fo'c'sle hatch and the canvas covers have not been lashed over the skylights.

In June 1894, before the start of a race on the Clyde of the Mudhook Yacht Club, the only day of the racing year when amateur helmsmen were permitted to handle the tillers of the big class, the *Satanita* collided with the *Valkyrie II* when trying to avoid running down a small spectator boat. As the yachts drifted apart the *Valkyrie II* sank, crushing William Brown of Rowhedge, one of her hands, when she ranged alongside the steam yacht *Hebe*.

The *Satanita* was repaired and continued racing for several years.

**3  Satanita**
*Satanita*'s first and second mastheadsmen checking the throat halyard. The peak halyard blocks are steel, and the men give scale to the housed top-mast and size of the masthead.

**2  Satanita**
Thirteen hands sheeting *Satanita*'s staysail as she surges along to windward.

**4  Britannia**
'*Britannia*, the pride of the ocean,' ran the old song, and in 1894, when this photo of Edward, Prince of Wales's racer was taken, it was appropriate for this fine cutter which over the years became a legend in yacht racing.

Her basic 10,000 square feet sail plan is supplemented by a well cut, long-luffed Yankee jib-topsail, set in place of the jib, which is set in stops beneath it with the jib sheets pendants and purchases hanging below its foot, ready to break it out when the jib-topsail is doused.

The 221 ton *Britannia* was a design of George Watson's firm; Clyde built, with wood planking on steel frames and beams, by D. and W. Henderosn of Glasgow in 1893.

Captain John Carter of Rowhedge, Essex, peers forward under the boom from the tiller. Thirty-one men are on deck, mostly from his village. The mate surveys the staysail luff as she slides along in the light breeze. A smaller staysail is bent to the forestay and lies stowed on the foredeck.

A smaller jib topsail is stopped down along the bowsprit, ready to send up if the breeze freshens and the big one is handed.

*Britannia*'s mainsail weighed 1½ tons and has eyelets for two laced reefs. A clew pendant is rove for the first reef which is flatted in by some reef points at the clew.

The mainsheet attaches to the boom with a strop instead of the multiple wire spans used a few years later, when sail areas increased by about 40%.

## 5  Lady Hermione

The yawl *Lady Hermione* was designed and built by Forrest and Son at Wivenhoe, Essex, in 1889, for the Marquis of Dufferin and Ava, a Victorian diplomat who owned several large yachts. His schooner *Foam* visited Arctic waters in the 1850s, resulting in his unusual yachting book *Letters from high latitudes*. For many years the Marquis's diplomatic duties prevented him from sailing in large yachts but in various countries he contrived to have specially built a small sailing yacht for single handed sailing, each embodying improvements until the *Lady Hermione* was built as his ideal single hander.

At first glance she appears a 'conventional' large yawl, but the size of her owner's head and shoulders gives scale to this 5 tonner, which he sailed and cruised until his death in 1902. She was 27 ft overall, 22 ft waterline length and 7 ft 3 in beam. The hull was composite-built with teak planking on galvanised steel frames and beams; a method favoured in large yachts and often used by Forrests for yachts of all types. She had watertight transverse and longitudinal bulkheads, making fore and aft peaks and two amidships wing compartments, which would keep her afloat if she were

holed. These were accessible by watertight flush hatches.

A 2 ton lead keel and some inside ballast ensured stiffness but she was too quick on the helm for the Marquis, who had a wooden keel fitted below the lead to allow him to work about the deck under way, in all weathers.

The Marquis was a practical seaman but incorporated so many gadgets in the little yawl that one visitor described her as 'something like the inside of a clock', though all had to be useable in any conditions.

The sails could be hoisted and lowered, the sheets worked, anchor be let go and weighed, tiller fixed in any position, without the solitary crew leaving the cockpit. Alternative wheel steering was arranged on the cabin top, to leave the cockpit clear when a lady passenger was shipped.

The tall, pole mainmast set an unusually narrow mainsail, staysail and topsail. The topsail has an uncommon feature in the brail leading around the leach just above the clew and through a thimble on the topsail yard. The mizzen, which has a similar brail to its luff, is loose footed and sheets to a jauntily curved bumkin.

The mainsail clew travels on a short iron horse. A steel wire rope ladder was fixed at the forward side of the mast, enabling the single-hander to get quickly to the crosstrees.

Brass fairlead sheaves at the foot of the mainmast led the halyards aft to a belaying pin rail across the after end of the cabin top, the falls being coiled in a rack of boxes on the cabin floor. As the *Lady Hermione* was rigged with the same number of ropes as a larger yacht, the owner had to deal with the main and peak halyards, two topping lifts, tack tackle and tack tricing line, topsail tack, sheets, halyards, and clew line, jib and staysail halyards and sheets, and jib and staysail downhauls. Each belaying pin had the name of its rope engraved on a brass plate. The mizzen halyards and lifts were similarly arranged at the aft end of the cockpit.

Ten, single lever, ratchet-barreled, 'gipsy windlasses' were used to hoist and sheet the sails and were portable, shipping into metal slides on deck when required. Four were used on the cabin top forward of the belaying pins: two on each side of the cockpit were used for the jib and staysail sheets, a couple of turns being kept around the barrel, with the fall belayed to a cleat when getting them in. When going about, these were first held

hand taut, then the ratchet handle was wound until the sheet was as taut as required, when it was belayed. This could be done in a few seconds and got the sheets flatter than the usual purchase. These are the first known use of 'sheet capstans' now called 'sheet winches', on board a yacht, though fishing vessels were using steam trawl capstans to trim sheets. Two winches forward of the mast were used for any purpose requiring a strong pull.

A long hawser was stowed forward of the mainmast as a tow rope for use in calms (the *Lady Hermione* had no auxiliary) when a steam launch or tug could be hailed. Rope guards were placed to avoid sheets fouling. The usual low footrail was supplemented by a guardwire and stanchions amidships. The cockpit could be completely covered by a large sliding hatch in bad weather, except for a small opening for the helmsman. In contrast, the cockpit also sported a fitting to hold a lady's sunshade in any position !

Unlike the elaboration on deck, the cabin was only fitted with a good sole, racks and cupboards for storage, and a mattress was spread on the floor for sleeping as the Marquis was a realist in small boat sailing. He shared his slumber with a 10 ft Berthon folding dinghy of wood and canvas.

The *Lady Hermione* was sailed during the winter, and on cold days the Marquis lit a brass charcoal stove under the cockpit grating; an arrangement of heating yet to be tried in modern yachts.

Although her equipment seems like an ingenious toy, the *Lady Hermione* was a very practical small craft of her time and the Marquis an accomplished sailor. He also owned the 75 ft gaff yawl *Brunhilda*, built at Cowes by Michael Ratsey as the *Lethe* in 1877, in which he 'went yachtin'' in a then conventional manner, but undoubtedly got most fun from the little *Lady Hermione*, which must, at that time, have been the smallest yacht to wear the burgee and white ensign of the Royal Yacht Squadron.

## 6 Aphrodite

The cruising schooner *Aphrodite* and her crew pose for a photograph in the mouth of the river Medina.

This shows the English cruising schooner yacht at her best. The clipper bow and standing bowsprit, a little dated when the photo was taken, and the bulwarks higher than in later yachts, but showing good freeboard and sheer, well raked masts and a beautifully seamanlike rig.

The owner, a guest, the captain and mates stand aft. The cook is amidships and 10 hands line the rail forward, one turning his back on the camera ! The carved figurehead and standing jib-boom point seawards, where this fine schooner belonged.

A small launch, probably a Li-Fu Company steamer, hangs from the amidships davits and the white gig, with bow badges, is typical of the fine boats carried by yachts of the period; planking in one length yellow pine on Canadian Rock Elm timbers with teak thwarts and bottom gratings, pulled by four hands to take the owner and guests ashore.

The lead of the standing and running rigging is worth study. The staysail and a jib are furled on the stays and coated. The spinnaker boom, topped up the foremast in yacht fashion, does not indicate racing ambitions, but a spinnaker would be set when passagemaking.

A happy photograph, copies of which probably hung in the owner's study and joined others in the 'front rooms' of her Solent area crew.

The 225 ton *Aphrodite* was designed and built by John Samuel White, the Cowes ship and yacht builders, in 1875, with principal dimensions of 110 ft 1 in length and 21 ft 11 in beam.

## 7 Aphrodite

A rigger's delight. The fore masthead of the schooner *Aphrodite*.

From below, the masthead supports the fore-topmast, held in wooden trestletrees by a metal fid at its lower end and at the masthead by the cap iron. Curved wooden spreaders are bolted to the top of the trestletrees to support the upper topmast shroud, which is notched into the tips. The inner ones are lodged in wooden thumbs further inboard. The outer ends of the spreaders are supported by a wire rope lift from the masthead.

The parcelled and served eyes of the foremast shrouds are led over the masthead, at the hounds, where they settle on the corresponding eyes of the starboard shrouds. The running backstay pendants lie under them and lead aft, served with white canvas so as not to mark the white foresail, when it is set.

The eyes of the inner and outer forestays lead around the masthead and rest on the lower part of the throat halyard 'crane', which in this yacht is 'A' shaped. A further eye is worked in them to pass clear around the heel of the topmast; all parcelled and served.

The masthead stay leads aft, between the fore and mainmast heads and above it the main topmast stay leads up at 45 degrees. Two pairs of topmast backstays lead down, aft from the fore topmast head.

The three-sheave, upper block of the foresail throat halyard hangs from the crane and the parts of the purchase drift down towards the throat block shackled to the stowed foresail gaff. The upper block of the foresail throat halyard purchase is visible a few feet below the throat block.

The three single-sheave blocks of the foresail peak halyard range up the masthead, the lower one fitted with a long arm to the shackle to hang the correct distance from the mast to clear the lead of the single part halyard. The small block at the eye linking the masthead stay and main topmast stay is probably a halyard for setting a topmast staysail.

The upper block of the staysail halyard hangs below the trestletrees and the forward spinnaker boom is topped up immediately forward of the halyards. The single-sheave jib halyard blocks lie one each side of the trestletrees and the outer jib halyard blocks hang from each side of the first mastband, below the masthead, with the single part halyard leading away forward to the block at the head of the stowed sail.

The topmast heelrope leads through a dumb sheave and a score hole near the heel, above the trestletrees, and up through a block at the masthead, ready to take weight off the fid and lower away when housing or sending down the topmast for maintenance, laying up, or to ease the vessel in bad weather at sea.

The block shackled to the masthead band appears to be one of a pair for the spinnaker boom lifts.

This fragment of a cruising yacht's rig indicates the amount of rigging work necessary when fitting out or laying up.

### Norman

The lee side of the 5 rater *Norman* 1895. T. Orr
Ewing, the owner, is at the polished bronze tiller,
under the watchful eye of the skipper, out of sight
on the counter. His wife and daughter sit on the
weather side of the shaped cockpit and one of the
two hands crouches in his racing position on the
side deck by the mainsheet, belayed on the cleat
under his foot a few inches from her surging wake.

### Egret

The 86 ft cruising schooner *Egret* reaches through
the Solent under full sail, 1898. She was designed
and built by Inman and Son of Lymington,
Hampshire, in 1859 and the square counter, clipper
bow and trailboards typify the period, though she
has a running bowsprit. The boat in davits carries
bow badges of her club burgee, in contemporary
fashion. She is tiller steered. The sag of a schooner's
narrow foresail is well shown here. Although its
boom is sheeted home the gaff sags to leeward
carrying the clew of the fore topsail with it.

For many years she was owned by G. A. Henty,
author of many adventure books for boys. He laid
the *Egret* up at Leigh-on-Sea, Essex, each winter;
one of the few yachts then maintained at this now
flourishing sailing centre.

## 10 Three cruising yachts

Three straight-stemmed cruising yachts about to tack off Cowes at the start of a handicap race, 1895.

The yawl nearest the camera is thought to be the *Sorceress* designed by J. Payne and built by A. Payne and Son at Southampton in 1878 as a modest sized cruising yacht. She occasionally raced in cruiser handicap events. She sports a jib-topsail and a well set jackyard topsail. The 35 ton *Sorceress* was 62 ft overall length, 51 ft 2 in waterline length and 13 ft beam.

Bulwarks of practical height, the anchor carried ready on them, just forward of the shrouds, the moderate length bowsprit and two rows of reef points in the staysail betokes the cruiser. The mainsail appears, somewhat unusually, to be laced to the boom and is reefed with lacings through eyelets in the seams. There are a few reef points towards the clew, probably to flatten the set of the reefed sail.

The mate, in blue guernsey and cheesecutter cap, is standing-by forward, quietly giving the 'All clear, Sir!' to the helmsman. A hand stands by the staysail clew and two others have set up the star-board running backstay and the shifting back-stay, further aft, ready to take the strain of the rig when she comes round. The helmsman, who in this instance could be the owner, has put the helm down and looks anxiously at a hand seated awkwardly in the boat on deck, handling the jib-topsail sheet. The skipper appears to be swinging aft from the runner tackle to assist him.

During 1976 *Sorceress* commenced refitting as a yacht after almost 30 years in a mud berth at Fingringhoe, Essex.

The white hulled cutter or yawl in the middle has a longer bowsprit on which a jib topsail is stowed. The black cutter to windward sets a smaller topsail of a type then out of fashion, having a short topsail yard setting at a considerable angle to the topmast and without a jackyard. These yachts have their racing flags lashed to the topmast heads, to ensure their flying vertical and true.

In the background the black ram bow of the battleship anchored as guardship looms before a large black racing cutter with a Royal Yacht Squadron burgee, which is possibly the royal racer *Britannia* Another large cutter with a racing flag aloft lies beyond her, in Cowes Roads.

## 11 Carina

The 40 rater cutter *Carina* close reaching in a strong wind, bursts across a Solent tide. Her speed under three lowers might be 9½ knots but, as with all sailing craft, the impression of speed created by the surging lee heel of her canvas and the jumping spray of the bow wave is tremendous. It was blowing hard when this photograph was taken as her topsail is not set. Short bowsprits were then fashionable in this class, which produced very keen racing as, despite the dazzling rebirth of the big class in 1893, the 40 raters were the largest numerical class racing all round the British Coast in the early 1890s.

The *Carina* was 60 ft 4 in waterline length, 15 ft 6 in beam and 13 ft draught. She set 3947 square feet. She was built in 1894 to the design of George Watson by D. and W. Henderson and Co. for Admiral Victor Montague.

The 40 rater class were principally sailed by captains and crews from the Essex river Colne, and when this photograph was taken the *Carina* was sailed by Captain Robert Wringe of Brightlingsea. Earlier she had been commanded by Captain Edward Sycamore, from the same port, who had previously sailed the *Corsair*. Brightlingsea also contributed Captain Tom Skeats in the *Creole* Captain Gould in the *Velzie* and *Varuna* and Captain Maskell in the German-owned *Irene*. From Rowhedge, up-river, Captain Lemon Cranfield sailed the *Corsair* in later years, Captain John Cranfield the *Lias* and Captain William Cranfield the *Caress*. Captain John Carter raced the *Thalia* and Captain Tom Jay the *Deerhound*, *Reverie* and *Thelma*. Against these were the *Queen Mab* sailed by Captain Ben Parker of Itchen, Hampshire and the Scottish *Isolde* raced by Captain Archie Hogarth from Port Bannatyne, Bute, both with local crews.

Unfortunately this photograph has been damaged but is a remarkable study of movement afloat.

## 12 Satanita

*Satanita* shows the power and beauty of the racing cutter rig as it had developed during the early 1890s. Captain Tom Jay of Rowhedge, stands at the tiller.

The jib topsail sheet always led naturally to the lee quarter, near the helmsman, set up and tended when racing by the cook and steward, who besides their duties below deck, had also to be good racing hands. The second mate stands just abaft the mast, in blues. The first mate and six hands are working on the foredeck and the remainder of the crew line the weather side. *Satanita* is close on the wind and the lee running backstay remains set up, but the shifting backstay, further aft, is slacked to allow for the movement of the boom. The mainsheet lies coiled on the counter.

The topmast is sprung forward against the pull of the mitre-cut topsail which spread 1470 square feet; almost the sail area of a 12 metre yacht. The mighty thrust of the gaff was countered by the horizontal jumper strut and its stay, giving extra support to the mast. The 5264 square feet mainsail weighed 1½ tons and the headsails spread 3360 square feet. Her boom is 91 ft long and height from the deck to the topmast shoulder 114 ft. She was timed to sail at over 16 knots off the Isle of Wight; the fastest cutter on a reach ever built. These figures give some idea of the size and power of these great yachts and the skill of their captains and crews when racing them in close competition against others of equal competence.

## 13 Satanita *(opposite)*

The racing cutter *Satanita* reaching across the camera lens. The balloon staysail, jib and jib-topsail are drawing well as she sweeps towards the next mark with the first and second mastheadsmen aloft on their usual perches, ready for anything.

The lead of standing and running rigging is well shown here. The shroud ratlines were not carried solely for convenience of the mastheadsmen, who often went aloft up the mast hoops under way, but were partly for use of the many hands needed to hoist the mainsail by going aloft, taking hold of the fall of the mainsail halyards to swing off to ride them down with their successive weight in a long line of men 'stringing down' as it was called, to help other hands hauling at the halyards on deck.

## 14 Britannia

*Britannia* reaches towards the next mark under 10,000 square feet of sail through a fleet of small yachts.

The mate and ten hands work on the foredeck preparing the spinnaker for the next run and the spinnaker boom is run forward in readiness. Four hands and the second mate overhaul the mainsheet on the counter. Jacketed guests in cheesecutters cluster amidships and Captain John Carter, crouching at her long white tiller, is visible between the guest in white trousers and blue jacket and another in blue.

Her sleek black sides reflect the frothing bow wave and shows her burnished bottom copper sheathing.

## 15 Britannia mast head

The first and second mastheadsmen alert at *Britannia's* masthead. One sits on the spreader and trestletrees, the other on the jumper strut, as she surges downwind. Soon they will be active, seeing the spinnaker lowers clear and possibly the jib-topsail hoisted.

It is interesting to compare the arrangement and lead of gear of this masthead with that of the large cruising schooner of Plate 7. The eye of the forestay lies above the band for the peak halyard lower block. The jib halyard blocks are steel, as is the starboard topping lift block, visible under the white, canvas-served runner pendant, near the hounds cheeks supporting the eyes of the shrouds.

The even tautness of the mainsail head lacing to the gaff is typical, but the gaff saddle appears to be very light to distribute the considerable thrust and movement of such a large sail. The spreaders are set up with standing lifts to the masthead cap iron and the topsail luff lacing can be seen passing around the masthead.

## 16 Meteor II

The German Emperor's racing cutter *Meteor II* reaching at speed, 1896. Despite the Kaiser's proud spread eagle racing flag, the *Meteor II* was British in most respects. Designed by George Watson and built by D. and W. Henderson at Meadowside, Glasgow, she was commanded and sailed by Captain Charles Gomes of Gosport, with a crew from Hampshire and the Isle of Wight, and Essexmen from the Colne. The *Meteor II* was a smart and fast yacht, well handled and winning a large share of the prizes for a few years.

The photograph shows her carrying a well setting yankee jib-topsail, a 'long roper', and a typical reaching staysail overlapping the mast by some 15 feet; a sail which had been carried in racing yachts since the mid 1880s and which appears to have been rediscovered when there was much fuss over 'invention' of the Genoa foresail in yacht racing during the 1920s.

There are more than 30 hands about the deck and Captain Gomes stands at the tiller, with the Kaiser's representative at his side.

Her speed can be judged from the bow and quater waves and the way the martingale is splitting the surface. She is probably making about 13 knots. The mainsail foot is secured to the steel tubular boom by a metal track and slides. A small jib-topsail is stowed on the bowsprit end.

The mainsheet and the peak halyard arrangements are worth study as each is distributing considerable strain from the 5500 square feet mainsail. The footrope under the boom end is to aid men when passing the reef pendants and the lacings for reefing or flattening the clew of the mainsail, on the 94-feet long spar.

The 8-inch footrails, almost low bulwarks, are typical of large racing yachts of the time.

The Kaiser subsequently had built three other Meteors, all large schooners and all being progressively manned with more and more German seamen training as racing yacht hands under English captains and crews, until by 1911 his *Meteor IV* had a crew almost exclusively German.

### 17 Meteor II

The after deck of *Meteor II*, on the wind. Captain Gomes at the tiller and 35 hands ready for the next move. The multiple part mainsheet attaches by wire rope spans to the 90-ft steel boom and has the usual footrope at its after end for the use of hands when reefing.

### 18 Race start, Cowes, 1897

The start for the Cowes Town Cup, Cowes Week 5 August 1897.

From right to left are Charles D. Rose's black cutter *Aurora* launched two months earlier and sailed by Captain 'Cook' Diaper of Itchen, Hampshire, with a Solent crew; the German Emperor's black hulled cutter *Meteor*, second of the name and a year old, sailed by the recently appointed Captain Ben Parker of Itchen with an all British crew, and the Prince of Wales's *Britannia* sailed by Captain John Carter of Rowhedge, Essex, with a crew from that village; all evenly matched first class cutters. They are closely followed by the slightly smaller *Bona*, owned by the Italian Duc d'Abruzzi, a noted mountaineer,

and sailed by Captain Edward Sycamore from Brightlingsea, Essex, with a crew from the Colne. Two 40 raters follow: the Scottish *Isolde* owned by Peter Donaldson and sailed by Captain Archie Hogarth and, well clear, Mr. Van Laun's *Caress* sailed by Captain William Cranfield of Rowhedge, with a village crew. She was designed by George Watson and was built by D. and W. Henderson at Glasgow in 1895 as a 40 rater, 64ft 5 in water-line and setting 4547 square feet.

The 175 ton cutter *Aurora* was designed by Joseph Soper and was built by J. G. Fay and Co. at

Southampton. She was an unsuccessful yacht which had a short life.

Seven hands lower away on her spinnaker boom lift while others tail on to the spinnaker halyard and a party aft trim the boom guy. The two mastheadsmen are standing on the spreaders to see the sail go aloft clear. Captain Diaper is at the tiller and the mate surveys it all from the foredeck. Beyond her, the *Meteor* has her spinnaker set and drawing, with most of the crew aft, sitting on the counter to obtain the best trim for running. The blanketed *Britannia* is just preparing hers.

With the spinnaker set each of these big cutters is carrying about 17,000 square feet of sail on one mast, handled by 35 men, remaining close to the yachting ideal of 500 square feet to one professional hand.

There are over 175 professionals at work in this photograph, captains and crews. Not an owner's hand on the tiller and many owners not on board, the captains being in full charge of the yachts throughout the long season racing around the British coast regattas, from May until September. In the foreground are two yachts' steam launches with spectators, including a lady in the larger launch whose hat and dress would now cause a sensation at Cowes.

It was a day of light, variable winds and at various times the *Aurora*, *Meteor* and *Isolde* led in the 50-mile course from Cowes, round the Warner Light Vessel to the east of the Isle of Wight, back to the Lepe buoy in the West Solent and then twice round these marks, to finish at Cowes. The *Aurora* finished in 5 hours 31 minutes 12 seconds, with the *Meteor* 6 minutes 5 seconds

before her, *Britannia* 54 seconds after her and the smaller *Bona* 6 minutes 32 seconds after *Aurora*: typical of the close racing amongst these professionally sailed and manned racers, even on a day of tedious winds. However, the race was won, on handicap, by the much smaller *Isolde* which finished 14 minutes 45 seconds after *Aurora*. Such mixing of first class with smaller racing yachts contributed to the temporary decline of large class racing in the late 1890s.

### 19 Moonbeam

The cutter *Moonbeam* anchored in Southampton Water for the photographer, displays the standing and running rigging of the type in silhouette. The bowsprit, with its bobstay and purchase to the cranse iron, and the lift leading through the port bulwark by the bowsprit housing, which would naturally be set up when at anchor to avoid the cable fouling the bobstay. The topmast forestay or jib-topsail halyards are set up to the bowsprit end. The staysail is neatly stowed on the foot of the forestay, at the stemhead, with its halyard purchase leading up to the usual anchorage for the upper block, under the topmast trestletrees.

The jib sheet with its purchase block and falls leads in through holes in the bulwark and immediately abaft these is the purchase for the port side bowsprit shroud, set up to the channel supporting the shroud lanyard deadeyes. The arrangement of the masthead fittings and details should be compared with those of the schooner in Plate 7, to see how standard was yacht practice at the time.

The spinnaker boom, topped up by its lift and set firm with a guy leading forward suggests that the *Moonbeam* occasionally raced.

The running backstays supporting the masthead are set up and show the pendant, span and purchase. The shifting backstays are set up to each quarter. 'Shifters' were usually fitted in three parts, as here, to allow their being led away forward and brought in to the shrouds and neatly set up when not in use. A pair of topping lifts supports the boom end, lodged in a scissors crutch, and the peak halyards are unshackled from the gaff spans and help to support the boom by a strop, and the stowed mainsail and its cover, which is neatly coated and laced tight around the mast.

Few things interrupted her flush deck; the hand capstan forward handled the chain cable; a small forehatch to the crew's quarters, in the fo'c'sle; a skylight over the saloon, abaft the mast; the main hatch to the accommodation, amidships; a small circular hatch to the sail and stores space aft, and the curved tiller.

Proportions, sail area and arrangements are typical of the type, as is the pleasant, sweeping sheer ending in a short, well tucked up counter. From the bowsprit end to the owner's burgee and the jauntily raked ensign staff, the *Moonbeam* exhibits every feature of efficient smartness then typical of a yacht, of a type which gave great pleasure to an owner and his family and friends, and summer employment to three seamen.

The 25-ton *Moonbeam* was designed and built by William Fife at Fairlie in 1858 and was about 52 ft long, 11 ft 8 in beam and drew 9 ft. She was extensively refitted between 1886–94.

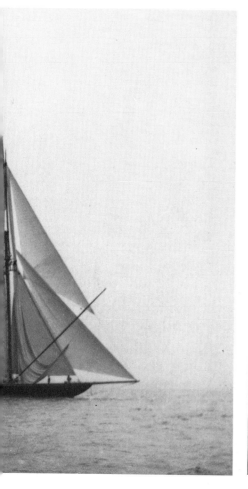

## 20  Moonbeam

This was the complimentary photograph taken for the owner of *Moonbeam* on the wind and, by chance, being passed by one of the Isle of Wight paddle steamers.

She has her balloon staysail, jib-topsail and a yard topsail set for the photographer, and the loose-footed mainsail has the puckering at the clew, often unavoidable with a white yacht mainsail. The three reefs are taken with a lacing and the eyes for this are visible in the vertical seams of the sail. She makes a brave picture with all hands 'lively'; Fred standing by the lee jib sheet under the foot of the foresail and Jim at the staysail sheets, while the captain kneels at the helm.

The rig and lead of all her sails and rigging are worth close study; it is all correctly set and arranged. This heeled view reveals the iron spreaders to the bowsprit shrouds.

The boat boom is stowed along the deck to port, rigged out from the side to keep the dinghy clear at anchor. The throat halyard is almost two-blocks. The mainsheet centre block has a buffer to take the shock of gybing. The mainsail clew travels on a short iron horse. The topsail yard is bending with the belly of the topsail, which causes the jackyard at its foot to bend in the opposite way. Unfortunately, the headsails are not of the best cut.

The skylights, compass binnacle before the tiller, and the circular lifebuoy lodged around it, are typical.

The crinkling surge of her bow wave is almost audible.

## 21  Moonbeam

This starboard side view of *Moonbeam* shows the topsail from the lee side, with its sheet led down through the lead or jewel block hanging from the throat of the gaff. The anchor and cable stowage is typical, except that at sea the bight of the cable would be caught up with a lashing.

## 22  Cowes fishing cutter

A fishing cutter hauling her shrimp trawl in the Solent. She was typical of the seventy or so small cutters owned at local ports and villages and fishing inside the Wight. Averaging from 17–22 feet length, these three-quarter decked craft were fast and able, built sometimes by yacht-yards and occasionally by shipwrights in their spare time. The carvel planked hulls were well formed and the simple rig was handy for trawling or dredging, which was their main use.

The owner, gathering the trawl on the quarter, wears the cheesecutter cap of the yacht skipper, and a white duck jumper. His mate has a yacht guernsey and most of the men owning and sailing these cutters were yachting all summer, returning in autumn to fit out for winter fishing.

The pair of sweeps on the foredeck would be used to row home in calms; the curse of the sailing fisherman's life.

## 23  Moonbeam's crew

Here *Moonbeam's* captain and crew of two hands post for their photograph. Such men were amongst the worlds smartest fore and aft sailors. Keen on their work and good at it, they were poorly paid for their ability. They were, generally speaking, a fine type of man, physically and mentally alert and taking as great a pride in their yacht as if she belonged to them. The captain of a cruising yacht such as the *Moonbeam* usually received about £2.10s. a week. The hands had 26 shillings weekly wage and 'found themselves' in food.

The arrangements of the channels, chainplates, deadeyes, lanyards and associated sheerpoles, the bowsprit shroud purchase and heel of the spinnaker boom are clearly shown.

## 24  Solent One-Design Class

The Solent One-Design Class racing out of the mouth of Southampton Water. The class appeared in 1897, when eleven boats raced, and was principally inspired by that indefatigable Solent day-racing owner Colonel Bucknill, who then wrote as 'Thalassa' in yachting journals; an experienced racing sailor and helmsman who owned a string of small racing yachts. He was captain of the class which was designed and built by White Brothers at Itchen Ferry.

Dimensions were 33 ft 3 in length overall, 25ft waterline × 7ft 9in beam × 5ft draught. Sail area was 750 square feet and displacement about 5 tons, with 2 tons 13 cwts of lead ballast.

Sails for the class were made by Ratsey at Cowes and were precisely similar in pattern, material and every detail, according to the sailmakers' instructions contained in the rules, which also allowed only one suit of sails per year.

A small jackyard topsail could be set above the mainsail. All boats carried sail numbers, then rather unusual, No. II being the Tangerine. No boat was allowed more than two professional hands when racing, when the owner or another amateur steered. The total cost of these boats, with extras, was about £210.

These fast and sporty little cutters were the equivalent to the present 'Daring' class yachts and provided as much close racing and excitement in their day. The canvas-covered decks of the flat sheered, low freeboard hulls glisten with spray raised by the rather lean bows, but the broad, flat counter eases the wake, as they heel to the freshening breeze clear of the spit. The small skylight and shaped cockpit are typical dayboat features, but the handy, pole masted cutter rig, with a short bowsprit, was unusual in a small racing class, then normally rigged with a large, high peaked standing lugsail and a single headsail tacked to the stemhead. The retention of the loose footed mainsail is also surprising, although practical as it enabled variation in the sails set to suit strong or light winds by adjusting the clew outhaul to flatten or throw belly into the sail.

Class stragglers are still fetching up towards the mark as the leaders are passing Calshot Castle, a stone fort at the end of the shingle spit off the New Forest shore, now fouled by old aircraft hangars and a lookout tower. A spritsail barge lies in the shallow bay backed by the gentle wooded shore of the edge of the Forest, now desecrated by a glittering power station and a sprawling mess of oil refinery wharves and installations.

## 25 Gadfly

The custom of flying prize flags was not confined to the large racing yachts, before 1939. Here the Solent One-Design *Gadfly* shows off her success in an end of season photograph, probably taken as she was on passage to one of the last races, towing her hack boat on a hazily fine morning with an easterly breeze.

The *Gadfly* gained 51 prizes that season, many of which would be firsts, the others seconds and thirds. In small yachts the flags were of the same size as the racing flag; in the large ones miniatures.

The owner is at the tiller. One of the two hands gives a pull on the staysail sheet while the other lies on the foredeck; both in passagemaking clothes – smart men who when the *Gadfly* laid up a few weeks later would be fitting out a little fishing cutter or seeking a berth in a steamship for winter employment.

The narrow yard topsail is, as usual, not drawing well on the wind despite careful setting, but reaching or running will add something to her speed.

## 26 Nevada

The American-designed 65-footer *Nevada* racing off Cowes 1901. *Nevada* was built that year for the 65ft rating class for Scottish owner P.M. Inglis to the design of C. F. Herreshoff, nephew of N. G. Herreshoff, who was then practising as a yacht designer in Scotland.

*Nevada* was short for a '65' and of very light, composite construction, with small displacement. She was fast in light weather but was unsuccessful principally because of her shortness. The *Tutty* was her only opponent, and sailed by John Connell was too good for her. These two were the largest yachts to make the round of the British Coast regattas that season, at a time when first class yacht racing was at a very low ebb. Her sheerline is unusual, the deck line at side appearing as a fair concave curve, but the top of the low footrail was flattened out to meet the sheer aft, saving windage and weight. The shallow and comparatively short counter contrasts with contemporary British practice. Her bow also appears remarkably full, though this is to some extent an illusion.

The sails are particularly interesting. The cross-cut mainsail seems full-cut to compliment the bending boom, but has a row of eyelets which enabled a foot lacing to flatten the sail when desired. The position and action of the leach battens is unusual.

The *Nevada* was very tender in anything but light winds and the mast, bowsprit, topmast and gaff were all changed for lighter spars within a month of launching. This probably reflected the designer's experience with yachts for American summer conditions. However, this is a good shot of a racer. One can sense the vibrant hum of her rig and the crisp wash of her passing as she slices in towards Cowes Green over the strong Solent tide.

## 27 Japonica

The yawl *Japonica* on the slipway, 1901.

During 1901 the *Japonica* was altered from sloop to yawl rig and appears here with her new masts, spars and sails with which, as a cruiser, she still spread 2540 square feet of canvas and remained fast.

Her double-skin mahogany planking retained its smoothness, and the plate fin keel, with its large bulb of lead ballast, and the balanced spade rudder, were features then common in smaller raters and are reappearing in new offshore racing designs.

The problems of slipping and cradling such craft are well shown, and the built up bilge blocks are typical, as is the apparent confusion of blocks, shores and sliding ways about the yard which, despite this casual appearance, were capable of excellent craftsmanship and was managed efficiently. It is however, surprising that a shore is not placed under her counter.

In the background, four shipwrights are working by a steam chest for steaming timber for bending. A two wheeled 'timber jim' for carrying logs to the yard for sawing stands near the open doors of a boatbuilding shed.

*Japonica* was built as the American 20 rater *Niagra* and was designed by Nathaniel G. Herreshoff for Jay Gould. She was built by the Herreshoff Manufacturing Company at Bristol, Rhode Island in 1895 to race in the 20 rating class, then popular in Britain. Her designer had no previous experience of this rule.

*Niagra's* captain was John Barr, a Scottish skipper of small racing yachts who had emigrated to America with his younger brother Charlie, who later attained fame as captain of several Americas Cup defenders.

Herreshoff cared little for conventional appearance but he insisted on good workmanship and efficient use of materials, but despite continual striving for reduction in weights, still designed a separate topmast.

During her season racing with the 20 rating class in British waters the *Niagra* was subject to protest from several British competitors who heard pumping from her each evening when at anchor, and suspected her of having water ballast tanks. Investigation revealed two bilge water tanks, filled and emptied by a pump and used for drinking water.

The *Niagra* was renamed *Japonica* and altered to yawl rig during 1901, and in 1908 a 4 cylinder Edge petrol motor was installed and she was converted to schooner rig of 2542 square feet.

After many years as a cruiser, she became a houseboat on the Heybridge-Chelmsford canal at Heybridge Basin, Essex, where her thoroughbred hull stood out amongst lesser craft. The *Japonica* left Heybridge under tow in the early 1950s, bound for somewhere in the Thames area, but is believed to have been lost on passage. So ended one of Nathaniel Herreshoff's most successful racers.

## 28 Rainbow

C. L. Orr Ewing's 331 ton schooner *Rainbow* setting her fore topsail before a race.

All hands are active as the group by the foremast prepare to set up the tack purchase and sheet home the sail. The bowspritendsman (an extra two shillings each week) is calling aft to the mate on the foredeck, probably warning of a craft standing across her bow. Captain Tom Jay of Rowhedge, Essex, stands at her tiller as she sails past an anchored smack.

The *Rainbow* was designed by George Watson and was built in 1898 by D. and W. Henderson at Glasgow, who constructed many large racers of composite construction, with steel frames, floors and beams, and longitudinal members planked and finished in wood. Her gracefully formed hull was 158 ft overall, 116 ft 3 in waterline length, 23 ft 10 in beam and drew 17 ft. She is here setting 13,400 square feet of canvas. Great care was taken in setting and trimming the well-cut cotton sails so these stood almost perfectly, and the size of the sails can be judged by the length of the topsail and jackyard of her maintopsail.

The *Rainbow* made her maiden passage from Gourock to Southampton in 50 hours and had the fastest timed speed for any displacement sailing yacht, sailing 60 miles in 4 hours, the log twice registering 16½ knots. Her principal opponents were the cutters *Satanita* and *Ailsa* both past commands of Tom Jay, and the *Bona* and *Aurora*.

Though *Rainbow* usually finished first, she did not win on handicap, which dulled the sport.

In 1902 she was sold to Verein Seefahrt of Hamburg and was renamed *Hamburg*, and continued to race in German and English waters, rating at 30.59 metres.

During 1905 the renamed *Rainbow* competed in the transatlantic race from Sandy Hook to the Needles, for the German Emperor's Cup. She raced against the *Sunbeam*, *Thistle*, *Ailsa*, *Fleur de Lys*, *Apache*, *Utowana*, *Atlantic*, *Hildegarde*, *Endymion*, and the ship-rigged *Valhalla*. The three-masted American schooner *Atlantic* won in 12 days 4 hours, and *Hamburg* (*Rainbow*) was second.

The magnificent *Rainbow* ended her days as a trading schooner to the Cocos Islands in the Indian Ocean, during the 1914-18 war.

### 29  Reindeer

The 85 ft cruising schooner *Reindeer* beats past Cowes under lower canvas. The square counter, bulwarks, clipper bow and bowsprit are typical of the 1860s. The *Reindeer* was designed and built at Lymington, Hampshire, by G. Inman in 1863 and was typical of many undistinguished yet well built yachts which gave pleasure to owners for many years after their launch.

The loose footed mainsail has four reefs and the foresail two, so she could be well snugged down and keep going in strong winds at sea. Cruisers of this size then regularly voyaged about the British and European coasts, to Norway and the Baltic, Spain, and to the Mediterranean, with the owner, his family and guests living on board for several months at a time.

Though less spectacular than serving in racing yachts the crew of a sizeable cruiser earned a steady wage, which with a Mediterranean cruise might last through a winter.

### 30  A cruising schooner

A fine unidentified cruising schooner reaching in the Solent.

Her skipper has the tiller lines at the lee side; a favourite position in fine weather, and the owner stands just forward of him. Two long-skirted ladies sit by the open skylight, which is probably over the 'ladies cabin', usually placed aft, and two men guests, correctly dressed in white trousers, pilot cloth jackets and cheesecutter caps, sit to weather. A hand stands by the mainsheet on the long, sweeping counter, by the little round hatch to the sail locker below, which was the use of that awkward shaped space in most yachts.

The differences in cut of the sails are worth notice, particularly the horizontal cloths of the well setting staysail. She sets a large, well cut jackyard main topsail, with a topsail yard long enough for a racing cutter.

Her skipper is obviously proud of her sailing and a vang is rigged from the fore gaff to flatten this tall, narrow sail and increase its efficiency, particularly to windward.

### 31 A cruising schooner's crew

Some of the schooner's crew pose for the photographer who recorded her grace and speed. The mate, in blue, sits by the lee bulwark, ever alert for craft ahead, and in charge of his foredeck. Two hands are in the white duck trousers and wear stocking caps, and two are in 'Shanghai', navy-style caps, while the cook/steward has a breather by the bowsprit in his white jacket.

The bow shape, decoration and foredeck arrangements were typical of about 1900. The martingale and lower bobstay is riffling through the water, emphasising her speed.

### 32 Oceana

*Oceana* was launched as the *Thais*, a topsail schooner designed and built at Cowes by C. Hansen and Son in 1880. She was an old-fashioned but graceful craft, well liked by her crews as a good sailer, and shows her speed in this photograph where she sets a big staysail on a reach but carries a small, jib-headed topsail above the loose footed mainsail, probably to preserve sail balance and ease the helm.

This 206 tonner was 123 ft overall × 21 ft 5 in beam and drew 12 ft 6 in. Sail area was 5830 square feet.

The *Oceana* had several owners during a long life. A pair of petrol auxiliary engines were installed in 1923. She made few long passages and cruised principally in British waters, in the English Channel and the North Sea. She was sailing until a few days before the outbreak of war in 1939.

## 33 Alexandra

The ketch *Alexandra* was built at Poole, Dorset in 1890 for the coasting trade. She had a plumb stem with small gammoning knee or 'Fiddle head' under the well steeved up standing bowsprit. Deep bulwarks set off her still graceful sheer, which ended in a shapely counter, though there is a hint of the shallow draught ketch barge in her hull. Potatoes from France and the Channel Islands, grain, stone, cattle foods and coal were her principal cargoes.

Numbers of similar ketches and schooners were built and owned at Poole and others sailed from many south coast ports; Rye, Newhaven, Shoreham, Littlehampton (where Harvey's yard built many), Portsmouth, Southampton, Cowes, Yarmouth (Isle of Wight) Weymouth, West Bay, Teignmouth, Salcombe, Dartmouth, and other places further west. The Poole vessels tended to be well found and smart sailers, and were soundly built.

When she finished trading, the *Alexandra*'s roomy hull attracted a yachtsman buyer and she sailed the English Channel under the burgee of Hamble River Sailing Club.

The camera caught her slipping along in a light fair wind under all sail. The mainsail had roller reefing, which was common in coasting ketches and schooners after the late 19th century, when crews were small. These gears were often operated by a wire pendant around a drum at the forward end of the boom, which had a stout gooseneck. The pendant, which might alternatively be of chain, was shackled to a purchase leading up and down the mast or along the deck. When this was tautened the drum and the boom revolved, reefing the sail as the halyards were slacked and a strain was kept on the topping lift shackled to the boom end.

The jib-headed topsail set on hoops to the topmast and was stowed aloft, lashed to the masthead and the shrouds. The loose footed mizzen had a flat cut and little roach to its foot; possibly a sail which drew well to windward, which few gaff mizzens will do.

An anchor would only be carried at the bow in calm weather or sheltered waters and was usually stowed fished up alongside the bulwarks.

The bowsprit net, boat in davits, accommodation ladder, ensign staff and flags were yachtsman's additions, but the *Alexandra* made a bold, purposeful cruiser, needing hard work and several hands for the pleasure she gave.

## 34 Glory

The view every racing skipper hoped to present to his rivals. *Glory* running through Spithead astern of two cutter rigged competitors, showing her immaculate topsides.

The mainsheet hangs slack in the light air, yet she slips along at probably 7–8 knots. British racing mainsails were then still cut with cloths parallel to the leach and this one has points for the first reef and lacing eyelets for the second and third.

The main jackyard topsail is cross-cut but the mizzen topsail has a diagonal seam.

The mizzen would make a large-sized mainsail for most present gaff rigged yachts, yet has only one point reef.

The vertical-cut spinnaker has its headboard almost to the block at the topmast head and the four part purchase forming its lift is shackled to a wire span. The spinnaker foot is creased against the outhaul.

A guy is set up from the head of the jackyard, down through a block on the main boom end, and is made fast along the boom to trim the clew of the topsail downwards and control the long, slender jackyard.

The 110 ft *Glory* was amongst the best and last designs of Arthur Payne, of Summers and Payne the noted Southampton yacht builders. She was built for Sir Henry Seymour King, with a generous rig. Captain H. Chamberlain of Brightlingsea, and his crew, revelled in her power and grace. She was a happy craft whose owner and his wife gave a dinner to the crew, on board, on their birthdays. During the 1904 season a hand was lost overboard and the owner vowed the *Glory* would not race again and she was sold, becoming the *Cassopeia*.

## 35 Shamrock I

*Shamrock I* thrashes to windward under 13,492 square feet of canvas.

In 1899 Sir Thomas Lipton made his first of five challenges for the Americas Cup with the *Shamrock I:* designed by William Fife, Junior, and built on the Thames by John I. Thornycroft and Co. noted as builders of steel torpedo boats, destroyers and special light craft. She was 128 ft overall length, 89 ft 8 in waterline length, 25 ft beam and drew 20 ft 3 in. The hull was flat and beamy, with long ends, and the keel was a deep fin, with great rake to the rudder at its after end.

Fife had designed many successful smaller yachts but had earlier only designed two large racers, neither particularly successful. *Shamrock*'s bottom was plated in manganese bronze, with side plating of aluminium. Her mast, boom and gaff were of steel. The mast gave constant trouble by bending in a breeze, impairing the set of her sails, of which she had six suits that season. She was commanded by Captain Archie Hogarth from Port Bannatyne, Bute, Scotland, who also had Captain Robert Wringe of Brightlingsea, Essex, to sail her in conditions favouring his experience. The practice of having two captains in Americas Cup challengers was a feature of the period 1895–1903 when the yachts grew so large and intricate that it was considered the experience of two men was necessary, and the possibility of one falling ill during the series also made it desirable. Her crew were Essexmen from the Colne, with others from the Clyde and Solent.

The *Shamrock* was beaten by the similar sized *Columbia:* designed and built by the Herreshoff Manufacturing Co. of Newport, Rhode Island, under the direction of Nathaniel G. Herreshoff who was amongst the world's greatest yacht designers and produced many defenders of the Americas Cup. The *Columbia* was sailed by Captain Charles Barr, a Scottish captain of small racing yachts then recently naturalised as an American citizen, who was to become a most noted racing yacht skipper. *Columbia*'s crew were from Deer Island, Maine, which then provided crews for many American racers; paralleling their British counterparts by fishing under sail in winter.

The races were held, as was then usual, in October off Sandy Hook, at the approaches to New York. *Shamrock* lost the first race, marred by fog, by 10 minutes 8 seconds. She lost her 56 ft topmast during the second race and had to give up. After protracted postponements due to fog, the third race provided a fresh wind but *Shamrock* lost by 6 minutes 34 seconds.

In 1901 *Shamrock I* participated in the British Racing season and acted as trials competitor for tuning up Lipton's next challenger, *Shamrock II*.

## 36 Shamrock I

*Shamrock I* starts to show her form, displaying all the grace and power of a large racing yacht.

Five hands prepare to set the jib topsail from the bowsprit end, supervised by the first mate on the foredeck. Several hands are trying gear by the lee rigging, with the second mate further aft. Captain Hogarth and Wringe, at the tiller, have discarded their pilot jackets and steer and comment on the race in shirt sleeves and waistcoats, as a concession to the magnificent summer day. As ever, the white clad mainsheetman stands alert at his post aft, by

the straining purchases and spans of his charge.

The jackyard is unusually far away from the gaff but the diagonal cut sail is setting beautifully and spreads almost 3000 square feet; considerably more than the sail area of a present 12 metre yacht.

Despite the elaborate rig, her designer still considered a fidded topmast necessary and it was not until *Shamrock II*, designed by George Watson two years later, that the lower mast and topmast were in one.

### 37 Shamrock II

*Shamrock II* seen here sail stretching and settling her rigging in the Solent, was designed by George Watson and was built by Dennys of Dumbarton, Scotland. Her side shell was plated in immadium, an expensive alloy of great strength for its weight.

She had two captains, both from Brightlingsea, Essex; Captain Robert Wringe is standing at the weather side while Captain Edward Sycamore is at the tiller lines. Both were great racing men.

The light air has not yet smoothed the wrinkles from her newly hoisted canvas. The mainsheetman stands aft, by the belayed fall, ready to ease it if ordered. Two hands stand to weather, having set up the shifting backstay on the quarter. The second mate, in charge of the after deck, stands by the rudder head, with a guest between him and Captain Sycamore. More guests are by the main-hatchway, close to the skipper, out of the way yet within reach for the brief conversation allowed from his concentration.

Amidships to port, several hands are preparing a sail to be set, probably a jib-topsail.

Two hands on the lee deck overhaul a tackle and a third coils the fall of the staysail sheet purchase, by one of the sheet capstans (which have since become popularly called sheet 'winches', though they in fact remain small capstans). The lead of the sheet is well inboard, emphasising the close sheeting angles of these large headsails.

The spinnaker boom, over 90 ft long, lies in its deck chocks and the upturned boat was carried by large racers to recover a man overboard, though this seldom occurred with these smart seamen. *Shamrock*'s crew could launch that boat, manned and pulling, in less than ½ minute, and two life-buoys were carried aft, ready to be flung to a man overboard. Great as was the danger of drowning, the stigma of having gone overboard during a race, causing the yacht almost certainly to lose her chance of a prize and her crew the prospect of prize money for that race, was (excusably) invidious.

A group of hands forward are hauling on a hal-yard under the eye of Charles Biffen, the mate at the mast, probably setting a jib not visible in the picture, as the great racer begins to show her paces in tuning up for her attempt at the Americas Cup against the *Columbia*.

### 38 Shamrock II dismasted

Just after the preceding photograph, *Shamrock II* lost her mast. Here 35 men are at work trying to clear the wrecked rig.

On the counter, Captain Wringe superintends work to haul up the broken jackyard and topsail, which was fast to the boom by the guy from the peak of the jackyard, via the lead block on the boom end. The boom is undamaged. The second mate crouches right aft and the first mate is report-ing from forward, by the tiller, where Captain Sycamore stands, undoubtedly angry and dismayed by the accident. The remaining danger is that the mast must be cleared from the bottom before the tide ebbs and the Southampton steam tug *Albert Edward* is in position ahead to keep the *Shamrock* head to tide and tow her clear when possible.

**39 Shamrock II dismasted (close-up)**

*Shamrock* dismasted in the Solent 1901.

The second mate sorts out some halyards, one foot on the boom, the other on the spinnaker boom on deck. The salvaged staysail lies on the foredeck where one of her hands and two of *Erin*'s men work at the broken gaff.

The light steel mast hoops are interesting and the gooseneck arrangements seem light compared to the sizes of mast and boom.

The falling mast does not appear to have damaged or distorted the side shell plating. A gang of platers were sent from a Cowes shipyard to cut it free.

**40 Schooner fitting out**

A cruising schooner fitting out in a mud berth at Cowes, Isle of Wight, 1898. The deep hull is copper sheathed below the waterline, as was then customary to keep a clean bottom. There is little difference in the height of her topmast heads but otherwise the rig is typical in proportion, arrangements and lead of gear. A squaresail yard is cockbilled on the foremast. The bobstay is drawn up on its lift. Her captain stands amidships and a hand is working at fitting out in his white duck jacket.

A chubby hulled cutter smack lies on her port quarter. Her stern shape, deep bulwarks and rig arrangements suggest French or Channel Islands origin. She has a chock pole shipped in place of the topmast, for winter sailing.

Steam yachts begin fitting out beyond, with others in berths at East Cowes, where a ketch airs canvas in the spring sunshine. A typical view of a yachting port stirring from winter sleep.

**41 Lisette**

The topsail schooner *Lisette* surges towards the camera under all plain sail, except for the gaff foresail, which is stowed.

The 116 ton *Lisette* was designed and built by C. Hansen and Sons of Cowes in 1873, with principal dimensions of 85 ft 6 in length, 18 ft beam, 10 ft 10 in draught. An auxiliary petrol engine was installed during 1908.

Her prominent channels, hawse pipes, trailboards and figurehead contribute, with the rig and the boats in davits, to the impression of a small sailing ship, rather than a yacht. The coiled line hanging from the bowsprit end is a gasket for stowing the jib on the bowsprit.

**42 Palatina**

The cruising ketch *Palatina* was one of the earliest large designs credited to Charles E. Nicholson of her builders, Camper and Nicholsons of Gosport, where she was launched in 1891 as the cutter *Guimili*. Her straight stemmed hull was 66 ft 6 in long, 14 ft 8 in beam and drew 8 ft 4 in. In 1903 she was re-rigged as a ketch, and an auxiliary engine was installed in 1926. She was a reliable type of cruising yacht, rather old fashioned at the time

Here she sets a fine spread of canvas including a balloon foresail and a pair of well setting jackyard topsails. The boats in davits are carried at the usual slight angle to keep the bows from catching spray, or the top of a sea in strong winds.

With a few other cruisers, the *Palatina* joined a menagerie class of large yachts during 1920 and raced on handicap against thoroughbreds such as *Susanne*, *Westward*, *Nyria* and *Britannia* but quickly returned to cruising.

## 43 Britannia

The royal cutter *Britannia* in cruising trim about about 1903 with the King and Queen on board for a day's sail in the Solent. The graceful shape of her hull was typical of the work of George Watson's office, which from 1885–1905 led a rapid development of hull form which, though now regarded as classic, was the basis of present thought and continuing endeavour.

The bowsprit was supported by shrouds and the rod bobstay by a martingale, which was fitted after the first season's racing in 1893. Robands attach the foot of the mainsail to the boom; a fine spar 92 ft long. The mainsail weighed 1½ tons, but the gaff was as light as possible. The jib and jib-topsail are drawing well but the staysail hangs limp and creased. The jib-topsail has a tack purchase to tauten the long luff and the spinnaker boom is topped up and down the mast out of the way.

Captain John Carter of Rowhedge stands at the long white tiller, typical of those used in large British racers until the early 1900s, when the American practice of wheel steering was adopted. In her period of use as a day sailing yacht from 1899–1912 the *Britannia* carried, besides her captain, a first and second mate and about 18 hands. For racing she needed about 32.

A hand on the counter stands by the mainsheet and another by the port shifting backstay, set up to the quarter to support the topmast head. The shackled joint in its length, half way up, allowed the lower part to be removed and stowed when the topmast was housed and the backstay was unnecessary. The running backstay is set up visually close to the mast.

A modest-sized, jib-headed topsail is set for the day's sail with ladies and guests on deck, and its luff lacing to the topmast is visible. The length of the gaff spans and lead of the halyards and blocks are worth study.

A well washed anchor is stowed at the rail ready to be let go as a kedge, if necessary during this light weather day. Her dinghy tows astern on two painters but will soon be hoisted in by the starboard side davits. The larger rowing cutter, usually carried on the port side, has probably been left at Cowes.

Ladies with long skirts and parasols and smartly dressed yachtsmen guests discuss the day with their royal hosts amidships. Others take the opportunity of a light breeze to look around the foredeck.

The King's flag as admiral of the Royal Yacht Squadron flutters from the topmasthead and the Squadron's white ensign droops from the peak. This photograph, more than any other in this book, typifies the peace, splendour and order of the Edwardian era.

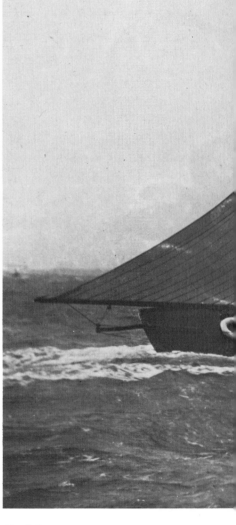

## 44 Saionara

The fast yawl *Saionara* heels to a breeze in 1908. She was designed and built for the 5 rating class by Charles Sibbick and Co. at Cowes in 1897, when he

was at the height of his ability as designer of fast, lightly constructed small racing yachts. The 5 raters were rigged either as sloops, with a high-peaked standing lug mainsail, or as gaff cutters.

In 1900 the *Saionara* was re-rigged as a yawl and was converted to a fast cruiser which was occasion-ally raced. She was the first command of Captain James Barnard of Rowhedge who later became noted as skipper of large racing and cruising yachts.

## 45 Wilful

The trim little cruising cutter *Wilful* slips by.

She was designed and built by Charles Sibbick of Cowes in 1899, 30 ft overall, 27 ft 6 in waterline, 8 ft 7 in beam and 5 ft 2 in draught. At one time she was renamed *Melody*.

The staysail foot, laced to a boom, is unusual and the slender main boom is bending under the close sheeting. The stocked anchor is catted, fisherman fashion, at the bow. Her pram dinghy was usually carried, capsized, over the skylight amidships as the chafing cover is shipped over the low bulwarks abaft the starboard shrouds.

A happy picture of a cruiser which wears the Royal Thames Yacht Club burgee and is still sailing from Burnham-on-Crouch, Essex.

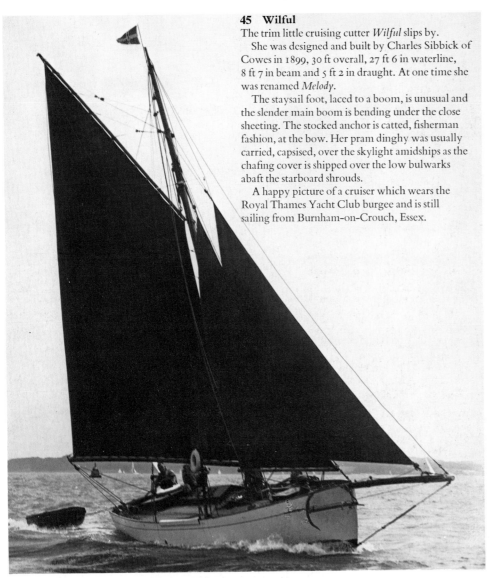

## 46 Valdora *(opposite)*

The Fife designed and built ketch *Valdora*, 68 ft 6 in waterline, reaching through Cowes Roads in the big handicap class, 1923. The spinnaker boom is run forward, hanging by its lift ready to be guyed out when the spinnaker is set at the next mark.

The 106 ton *Valdora* was built in 1903 and was rigged as a yawl. She was sailed by Captain Button and a crew from the river Colne, who had great rivalry with the similar lovely yawls *White Heather* and *Brynhild* and particularly with the *Leander* built by Summers and Payne at Southampton; an 80 footer with a Solent crew. These fast yawls expressed the striving of owners for more wholesome yachts than the lightly built and oversparred craft to which the contemporary rule makers had driven the sport.

*Valdora* won the German Emperor's Cup, racing from Dover to Heligoland in 1904, beating the 248 ton American schooner *Ingomar*, sailed by the Scotch-American captain Charles Barr, the 100 ft racing yawl *Navahoe* and others of a fleet of large racers, which went roaring and rolling away up the North Sea, carrying Solent racing canvas in a strong wind.

In the following year she finished third in the Royal London Yacht Club race from Cowes to the Clyde, won by *White Heather*.

In 1912 she was re-rigged as a ketch setting 5563 square feet and passed to the ownership of Sir William Portal, who used her mainly in the Solent.

By 1923, the *Valdora* was racing with a revived big class, including the royal *Britannia*, *Nyria*, *Terpsichore* and her near sister, the ketch *Cariad*. Later she was owned by F. Rees. She was a yacht well liked by her crews, who recalled her seaworthiness and handling with affection half a century after she was launched.

## 47 Edie II reaching

The 36 ft linear rater *Edie II* on sailing trials, 1905. This class approximated to the later 8 metres of the International Yacht Racing Union rule, established in 1906 for yachts of 5, 6, 7, 8, 10, 12, 15, 19 and 23 metre classes.

The *Edie II* was designed by Arthur E. Payne, junior and was built at Southampton by Summers and Payne, noted builders and designers of many beautiful, fast and noted yachts, for racing and cruising.

There are no battens in the leach, which is flapping. The peak halyard and gaff span arrangements are unusual but effective. A topsail could be set from the pole masthead.

During sailing trials it was customary to wear the ensign at the peak and the owner's burgee at the truck, if he was on board, as though the yacht were cruising. The low freeboard and streaming decks evoke the speed of the rater classes and *Edie II* has the clean look of efficiency in hull and rig

**48 Edie II, cockpit**
When Roger Smith enlarged part of the *Edie II*
photograph he discovered this group in her cockpit; the informally dressed owner at the tiller
with his skipper, two hands and a friend, sheltering
to windward during trials. The sheeting arrangements are interesting in this large dayboat. The
running backstay is set up by a Highfield lever,
then recently designed by J. S. Highfield.

**50 A 6 metre at speed**
A gaff rigged 6 metre at speed. From her racing
flag to the then fashionable spoon bow forced by
the rating rule, she portrays the speed and exhil-
aration of yacht racing. Most of this class, and the
similar 7 metres, set the single headsail to the stem
head.

A large reaching foresail is stowed on the slip-
pery, varnished foredeck. The long gaff of the
cross cut mainsail is sagging slightly in the fresh
breeze as she slices across the tide, the lee wash
licking close to the coamings of the large cockpit.

### 49 Corona and Octavia

19 metres sweep across Spithead in 1912.
R. Hennessy and A. Paget's *Corona* C.3, leads
William Burton's *Octavia* C.2, in close racing
typical of this class, which were long regarded as
the finest moderately large racing yachts ever built.
Both were launched in 1911 and cost about £6000.

*Corona* was designed and built by William Fife
and Son at Fairlie, on the Clyde. *Octavia* was
designed by Alfred Mylne and was built at
Dumbarton by McAlister. Both exhibit the cutter
rig in its most graceful beauty and sense of speed
and power.

*Corona* is sailed by Captain Stephen Barbrook of
Tollesbury, Essex, with a crew from that village
and the Colne. Hard on his heels is William Burton
at the wheel of the *Octavia*, with his skipper, Captain Albert Turner of Wivenhoe, Essex, by his
side, a Colne crew itching to beat their rival, and
mate Charles Wadley at the stemhead, watching
*Corona*'s every move.

They were amongst the smartest crews in
Britain and their rivals were the Fife designed
*Mariquita* sailed by Captain Sycamore of
Brightlingsea, Essex, with a Colne crew, and the
Nicholson designed *Norada* which had a crew of
cruising hands, yet went wonderfully. All were
relatively good sea boats, making some hard
passages around the coasts to the racing fixtures and
to the Baltic regattas.

*Octavia*'s dimensions were 95 ft 3 in overall,
62 ft 3 in waterline length, 17ft 11½ in beam and
11 ft 11 in draught. She displaced 72½ tons and set
6216 square feet in a rig having a total height of
117ft above deck; low compared with the larger
class racing cutters. The mainmast was 14 inches
diameter at deck. The 71 ft 3 in boom was 12 inches
at centre and extended 14 feet beyond the counter
and the 9 inch diameter bowsprit extended 17 feet
outboard from the stemhead.

The wide spreaders and baby jib-topsails are
worth study. The wonderfully flat setting jackyard
topsails are bending the peak of the topsail yards
slightly and have the mitre seam leading horizont-
ally from the heel of the jackyard, to keep the lower
part well set. The spinnaker booms are run forward
to be ready at the next mark.

Before 1914 the metre classes carried sail
numbering in a system of distinctive letters for
each class, commencing with A for the largest and
extending downwards, in order.

## 51 Jeano

The 15 metre class cutter *Jeano* at maximum speed, 1912.

The 15 metre class was established by the International Yacht Racing Union conference of 1906, as successor to the 52 ft class of the previous rating rule, which in turn descended from the 20 rating class of the 1890s and the earlier 20 tonners. So this fast cutter had a long lineage of usually fast and successful yachts, which provided good sport.

The *Jeano* was built at the *Tritonia* by Alexander Robertson at Sandbank, Scotland, in 1910, to the design of Alfred Mylne. She was unsuccessful in early races until John Cranfield of Rowhedge, one of a noted family of Essex racing captains, sailed her, and she started winning prizes.

Her bow and stern waves are scoring across the swift Solent tide with a competitor close astern and to weather, barely visible under *Jeano*'s boom. The flattening effect of her after lines and the counter shape is particularly interesting at this speed.

The forestay has moved aft and the bowsprit is shorter than in older yachts of the class, but she still carries a topsail yard on the diagonally cut topsail.

The 15 metre class effectively ended in 1914, though individual yachts, such as *Cestrian* and the *Lady Anne* continued racing during the 1920s.

## 52 The 15 metres class

A fleet of 15 metres running into Cowes Roads in 1913, *Jeano* D.3 in the foreground.

These yachts were a fine class of slightly larger size than the present 12 metre class but setting twice as much sail and needing a crew of eight.

The German owned *Sophie Elizabeth* D.6, is ahead of *Jeano*, *Hispania* D.5, *Paula III* D.8, and *Mariska* D.1, are holding course inshore and appear to have gained by it.

*Paula III* was designed and built by Camper and Nicholsons Ltd. at Gosport in 1913 for Herr Ludwig Sanders. She was a very successful yacht, raced that season by Captain Edward Sycamore of Brightlingsea, with a Colne crew.

The *Hispania* was designed by Fife and was built in Spain by Astilleros Karrpard at Passages in 1909, for King Alphonso, who was fond of yachting. Like the Germans, the Spanish King came to England for his racing yacht captains and crews, and *Hispania* came out sailed by Captain Steven Barbrook of Tollesbury, Essex. Later she was sailed by Captain Robert Wringe of Brightlingsea. *Hispania* was 76 ft 2 in overall length, 48 ft 5 in waterline, 13 ft 9 in beam and drew 9 ft 4 in. She set 4300 square feet in her cutter rig and was typical of this fine class. Her dismasted hull lies at West Mersea, Essex, as a houseboat.

*Jeano* gives a good impression of the crowded deck of a modest sized racer. The skipper at the tiller discusses the race with the owner kneeling on the deck beside him, and the mate and guests sit on the counter to keep as much weight aft as possible. A guest in cheesecutter and white trousers assists two hands to prepare some gear. Things are relatively relaxed on board but this will change dramatically at the next mark.

The spinnaker boom lift hangs slack but is ready for lowering at the mark. Three hands stand by the boom, two attempting to hold it down and improve the set of the skying spinnaker. The running and preventer backstays are set up to weather. The mainsail does not set well off the wind, though no doubt its creases largely disappeared when the sheets were gathered for windward work. The gaff and its saddle seem light for the mainsail area. The length of the single spreaders is well shown and the shorter intermediate spreader for the masthead stay was socketed to the mast below the gaff saddle after the mainsail was set.

## 53 Minna Dhu

The rakish little cutter *Minna Dhu* was successful in the small handicap classes from her lauch in 1909 until the 1930s, which is not surprising as she was designed by Arthur Payne and built at Southampton by Summers and Payne as a fast cruiser, suitable for handicap racing.

The 10 ton *Minna Dhu* set 1000 square feet on hull dimensions of 42 ft 6 in overall length, 30 ft waterline length, 8 ft 3 in beam and 5 ft 5 in draught. Her shallow hull body resulted in an unusually high and long cabin top to provide accommodation when cruising and for the racing crew. Unfortunately, this left little clear deck room, particularly important in a yacht when racing, and the foredeck is cluttered by the circular forehatch.

Great sport could then be had with a fast yacht of this modest size, cruising along the south and east coasts and racing in the regattas, with the owner at the helm, and a crew of friends, and one well trusted hand to produce the beef and back-up to the keen owner.

Here *Minna Dhu* is sliding along windward with a small jib-headed topsail set above a single reefed mainsail, although only a small jib and working staysail are set, she carries a jib-topsail which is not standing well so close hauled on the wind. Her rig was a miniature of the larger racing cutters. Low freeboard and little sheer made these fast cruisers wet, but their concept and use are interesting in any period.

## 54 Mandy

The 26 ft centreboard yawl *Mandy* stealing into Cowes on a summer evening in 1925, through the Roads crowded with anchored yachts, against a workaday background of spritsail barges.

*Mandy* was designed and built by her owner, Major H. A. Pratt, at Parkestone, on Poole Harbour, Dorset, in 1913, at the height of popularity of small, pointed-sterned yawls, influenced by the designs of artist-yachtsmen such as George Holmes and Albert Strange of the Humber Yawl Club, whose members were notable in small boat cruising.

The *Mandy* set 367 square feet in mainsail, mizzen and single headsail set on the invaluable Wykeham-Martin furling gear. The high-peaked gaff mizzen would contribute little to her sailing efficiency and would have been better as a triangular 'leg of mutton' or Bermudan sail.

In those days cheesecutter caps and white guernseys were normal wear in even such small yachts and she wore the burgee of the Royal Thames Yacht Club. In later years she was owned at Falmouth.

## 55 Ivernia

The Dutch 'Klipper' yacht *Ivernia* was built as the *Heralda* by G. De Vries Lentsch at Nieuwendham, Holland, in 1922. The 58 ft 4 in hull drew only 4 feet and 15 ft 1 in beam assured stability for her 1700 square feet cutter rig.

The 'Klipper' yachts developed from the cutter and ketch rigged cargo carriers of the Dutch coast, estuaries and rivers, which also voyaged to the Baltic and occasionally to England.

Klippers were usually built of iron or steel and had almost flat bottoms, well rounded bilges and

straight sides. The bow sections were either slightly rounded, as here, or flared, and many had considerable sheer. The elliptical stern is typical, as are the fresh water shaped leeboards and the topping bowsprit. The cutter rig and yard topsail are of yacht proportions and the long coachroof indicates she was built as a yacht.

These craft are useful and spacious for shoal water cruising, ideal for the coasts of Essex and Suffolk, or similar waters, capable of taking the ground upright and of standing a reasonable amount of bad weather, but dull sailers to windward in a short sea.

The name 'Klipper' is believed to have been adopted in imitation of the square rigged fast clipper ships of the mid 19th century, when this Dutch type probably originated.

## 56 Citara

The 12 ton cutter *Citara* was built as the *Rover* by Robert Aldous of Brightlingsea, Essex, in 1887 for G. M. Coxhead. She was typical of scores of small cruising yachts built at the time, many of which were long-lived.

Aldous was noted for yachts of this type, large and small and most resembled the Colne cutter smacks, whose building kept Aldous busy for many years, and the yachts and the smacks interacted on each other's development over a long period as the same local seamen skippered and manned each in season.

The *Citara* is 36 ft overall lenght, 32 ft waterline, 9 ft 8 in beam and 6 ft draught. Her rig spreads 931 square feet.

This is how she looked in August 1938. She is now owned by B. C. Munden of Portsmouth.

## 57 Pastime

The little Solent fishing cutter *Pastime* reaching into Cowes with a quartering wind on a summer's day in 1923. From the fine mesh beam trawl protruding over her quarter she appears to have been prawning or shrimping. The *Pastime* was typical of the many small fishing cutters working from Cowes, Wooten Creek, Lymington, Pitts Deep, the Hamble, Portsmouth, Gosport, Itchen village, Eling, and Hythe until the late 1920s. These transom sterned, carvel planked craft drew up to 4 ft, but more usually about 3 ft 6 in, and the beamy, well formed hulls were fast and carried most of their ballast inside. The foredeck and bulkhead enclosed a two berth cuddy, the remainder of the boat being open. A wooden fish tray or culling board went across the after end, and trawls and dredges were emptied into this, if possible, to avoid fouling the undecked boat.

Sail areas were generous, though few carried a topmast or topsail. A variety of jibs were set. The single part peak halyard is unusual.

The crew of two men or man and boy were usually yacht hands in summer and fishermen in winter, but a few, like *Pastime*'s owner, fished the year round. These inexpensive little cutters were built in yachtyards or by shipwrights in their spare time. Many were designed by skilful local yacht designers, such as Arthur Payne, and were fast for their size.

Races for the various classes of fishing boat were held at local regattas, champions being Sam Randall's *Freda* of Hythe; William Bevis's *Oyster* of Bursledon; George Parker's *Dragon* from Itchen; Bob Edward's *White Belle* of Hamble; Dan Cozen's *Gazelle* of Weston; and Joe Oatley's smart *Harriet* from Cowes, and others.

The *Pastime* is still working for a living under power from Cowes, with the stump of her mast rigged with a derrick and a wheelhouse set into her foredeck.

## 58 Dolly Varden

Thomas Ratsey's *Dolly Varden* slips over a Solent tide under her well setting, tan sails. She was descended from the Solent fishing cutters. In 1872 Mr Grant, then secretary of the Royal Yacht Squadron, admired the fast, 21 ft fishing cutter *Star* built in the 1840s at Itchen village by an unknown shipwright. Mr Grant had her lines taken off and enlarged and the yacht *Dolly Varden* was built from them; 36 ft 10 in overall, 35 ft 6 in waterline length, 11 ft 3 in beam and 6 ft 6 in draught. She set 1662 square feet in the cutter rig. She was raced in charge of Mr Paskins, owner of the *Star*.

In 1888 the *Dolly Varden* was sold to T. W. Ratsey of the sailmaking firm, who admired her, and continued her performance as a small handicap racer for the next half-century, during which she carried beautifully setting sails, and many innovations in sailmaking were tried and perfected on board her. In this photograph she carries a tall, Marconi rig which needs two spreaders to stay it. The tan canvas sails set to perfection.

Throughout her long and successful life the *Dolly Varden* was regarded with affection as the heroine of the Solent fishermen and yachtsmen.

## 59 Moonbeam

Many thought large yacht racing would never revive after the First World War but at the end of 1919 King George V decided he would race the *Britannia* during 1920 and this lead brought spectacular results. The *Terpsichore* was ordered by R. Lee, *Nyria* was bought by Mrs Workman and emerged as the first large racer with Bermudan rig, sailed by Captain Bob Diaper of Itchen, Hampshire.

Sir Charles Allom bought the 23 metre *White Heather II* (Plate 82), *Westward* fitted out under Captain Sycamore, the racing schooner *Susanne* joined in, and Charles Johnson ordered the 93 ton cutter *Moonbeam* from William Fife, to be sailed by Captain Tom Skeats of Brightlingsea, Essex.

Here *Moonbeam* runs under spinnaker with the baby–jib topsail set in stops, ready to break out. She was a moderate sized racer, 95 ft 4 in overall length, 16 ft 8 in beam and 12 ft 3 in draught.

The sunken deckhouse amidships has its canvas cover rigged to protect the varnish and the endings of the caveata line at the sheer show the dragon head and tail which was Fife's trademark after the success of a series of their designs named *Dragon*, during the 1890s.

## 61 Moyana II

Battle of the rigs. Wilfred Leuchar's gaff sloop rigged *Moyana II* ahead but to leeward of Thomas Sopwith's Bermudan cutter rigged *Doris* in a 12 metre class race, 1925.

The *Doris* was new that season from Camper and Nicholsons' Gosport yard. *Moyana II* was designed by Alfred Mylne and was built by the Bute Slip Dock Co, at Port Bannatyne, Bute, in 1924. Her rig of 2800 square feet exhibits the final phase of the gaff's stand against the increasing efficiency and acceptance of Bermudan rig in racing. The Marconi mast and topmast are combined in one tapering hollow spar, the gaff is at optimum peak for a well setting mainsail with topsail above, and the boom length is moderate. The luff of the diagonal-cut topsail is carried on a track, with a lacing drawing the lower end to the mast and a jackyard extending its foot, and bending under the strain on the sheet.

The single headsail is unusual with the gaff racing rig, most contemporary yachts being rigged as cutters, with staysail and jib, and it reflects the influence of the majority of the class, then turning to the Bermudan sloop rig.

*Moyana II*'s skipper sits on the lee side advising the owner at the tiller. Out of sight, on the weather deck, are her three hands, only four professionals being allowed in a 12 metre.

The late 1920s and 1930s brought the 12 metre class to its finest pitch, racing at regattas around the coast. The boats cost about £4500 and provided owners with most of the thrills of big class racing at the expense of a modest crew. These 70 ft sloops were allowed to set spinnakers of up to 3000 square feet area, which were difficult to handle with a professional crew of four.

## 60 Sumurun

The 92 ton yawl *Sumurun* reaching through the Solent during a handicap race.

The *Sumurun* was designed by William Fife as a fast cruiser and was built at Fairlie, for Lord Sackville by W. Fife and Son in 1914, being launched in May, and was just able to show her form in handicap racing before war commenced.

She and the similar yawl *Rendesvous*, built by Fife a year earlier, formed an excellent type of yacht, setting 5580 square feet, large enough to be fast and able at sea, yet capable of being sailed by a skipper, mate and 10 hands.

A nice touch, typical of the way she was raced, is the use of a second racing flag set clear above all on the head of the topsail yard, rather than relying on the often distorted wind direction given by the racing flag at the topmast head.

For many years *Sumurun* was sailed by Captain Gurten of Tollesbury, Essex, who later made his home at the Suffolk waterside village of Pin Mill, where he retained his love of wildfowling to the last.

Here he is by the wheel, leading the handicap fleet on a summer's day and no doubt chuckling over how he has got ahead of the *Rendesvous*, sailed by his friend Captain Jim Barnard from Rowhedge, Essex.

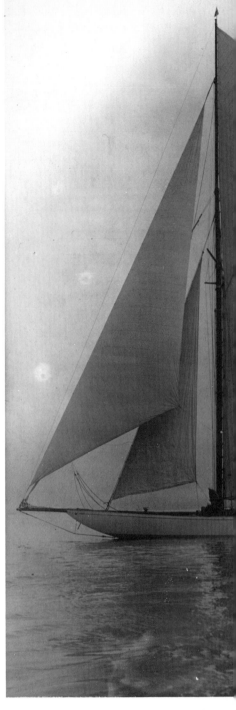

## 62 Winflower

*Winflower*, X one-design class boat number 4, reefed in a breeze off Yarmouth, Isle of Wight, 1924, when the class was rigged as gaff sloops.

She carries a small roller foresail and the roller reefed mainsail is well set. A. Westmacott designed these keelboats which are 20 ft 8½ in overall, 17 ft 8½ in waterline, 6 ft beam and 2 ft 9 in draught and carry 200 square feet of sail, nowadays in Bermudan sloop rig.

There are now strong fleets at Cowes, Yarmouth, Lymington and the Hamble river, with others at Poole, Weymouth and Chichester Harbour. Several hundred boats race each season and they form the largest class at Cowes Week.

The X class is one of the finest small keel boat classes; handy, roomy and fast, able to race in strong winds and a sea; safe, and above all comfortable for families to race or go off sailing for the day.

One can regularly see dozens starting in weekend races, or individual boats anchored in quiet Solent creeks; the owners and their families picnicking and bathing. The class is still built in numbers by Clare Lallow of Cowes, with traditionally excellent finish.

## 63 June

The 50 ft 5 in waterline cutter *June* sets 3458 square feet in this cutter rig.

*June* was designed and built in 1905 by William Fife and Son at Fairlie, Scotland, as the yawl *Gelasma*. Later she was renamed *June*, *Candida* and *Uldra* (in French ownership), before reverting to *June*. Converted to a yawl and then back to a cutter in 1923, she raced with success in the 30–70 tons handicap class until the 1930s.

Here the owner is at the wheel, seated with a guest on the steering gear casing. The skipper tends the mainsheet on the counter and her hands line the lee side in an attempt to keep the sails drawing in the near calm.

A jib is set in stops under the 'long roper' jib-topsail and the small staysail is probably set to

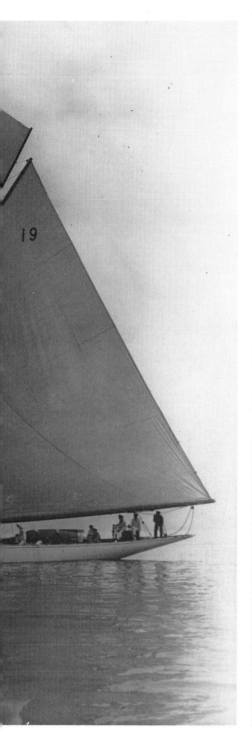

avoid interference with the mainsail in light airs. The diagonal-cut Marconi topsail is drawing, set to the masthead on a track, with the clew spread by a jackyard.

Marconi topmasts were introduced with the Nicholson designed 15 metre *Istria* built for Sir Charles Allom in 1911. To save weight the functions of lowermast, topmast and topsail yard were combined into one long, tapering mast, whose light and elaborate standing rigging caused it to be known as a 'Marconi', after the Italian inventor of wireless, then becoming prominent. The rig quickly spread to most moderate sized racing yachts and was used in the larger cutters during the 1920s.

*June* has the gaff cutter rig in its final development for racing.

**64   Iyme II**

*Iyme II* thrashes past Yarmouth pier under a well roller-reefed mainsail, staysail and storm jib on the invaluable Wykeham-Martin furling gear, run half way in along the bowsprit.

This shows the Marconi topmast rig's windage in a strong breeze, which sets her topsail sheets and ensign halyard flying as *Iyme II* tramps on, racing to the westward.

## 65 Water Witch II

*Water Witch II*, a reefed Solent Sea Bird one-design class boat gets up and goes in a puff off Yarmouth harbour, 1924. These centreboard 18 footers were designed and built by H. Gale at Cowes in 1900, for members of the Solent Yacht Club. With 6 ft beam and buoyant hull form they carried 200 square feet in mainsail and foresail. These were good sea boats, often used single-handed for day sailing, and competing in weekly races throughout the season.

Small boats of this general type were the popular local classes before national and international dinghy and keelboat classes largely displaced them during the 1940s and '50s, though most were rigged with a high peaked lug and later a Bermudan mainsail and a foresail, rather than a gaff rig. These boats had a generous sail area and an unusually long bowsprit to spread the roller furling foresail, which is tacked to the end of a spinnaker boom capable of being swivelled out at right angles to the centreline so the foresail became a spinnaker for running, a feature common from the 1890s to 1920s.

The halyards are all led aft via sheaves at the foot of the mast, to belay in the cockpit.

The roller reefing mainsail has drooped and the topping lift has been set taut to keep the boom clear of heads when in stays, and the mainsheet from fouling.

There is a great sense of the power of wind in this photograph, which almost transmits the throbbing vibration of the tiller and surge of the lee side.

## 66 Water Witch II

*Water Witch II* running with her roller foresail boomed out and a well reefed mainsail.

### 68 Jolie Brise

E. G. Martin's ex-Le Havre pilot cutter *Jolie Brise* becalmed in the Fastnet Race, 1926.

The Le Havre pilots cruised seaward in a series of bold cutters, most of which were built there by M. Paumelle. The *Jolie Brise* was launched in 1913 at the peak of development, 56 ft overall length from her plumb stem to the short, well tucked up counter; 48 ft waterline, 15 ft 9 in beam and 9 ft 6 in draught. She set over 2200 square feet in the working rig and here carries a fine, light spinnaker and a jackyard topsail. An auxiliary engine was installed in 1927 and she was afterward sold to a Mr Mortimer.

Martin was one of the great fore and aft seamen of this century, owning light displacement, Bermudan rigged yachts as well as this husky cutter, and seafaring in many types of sailing craft including a winter spent voluntarily as mate of the Ipswich sailing barge *Vigilant*. He understood small sailing vessels and the men who manned them for a living. They respected him and he learned much from them. He is now often remembered as a founder of the Royal Ocean Racing Club and as a keen participant in early British offshore events during the 1920s and 30s. The *Jolie Brise* is still sailing under Portuguese ownership.

### 69 Jolie Brise

Here, in contrast, is the *Jolie Brise* under tanned canvas and setting a jib-headed topsail. The bold bow, sweeping bulwarks and ample freeboard are hallmarks of the French and English pilot boat types.

She is competing in an offshore race, 1929.

**67  Tessa** *(far left)*

The 25 ft waterline cutter *Tessa* was typical of the hundreds of smaller yachts which give great pleasure at modest cost. Her hull form appears to be similar to the Solent fishing boat type.

She is racing in a handicap event and the amateur crew have just set the spinnaker as she squares away through Cowes Roads.

**70  Amaryllis**

The yawl *Amaryllis* at the start of an offshore race in the 1920s.

The *Amaryllis* which was for a time named *Conquest* was designed by W. F. Baynes and was built by A. Payne and Son at Southampton in 1882 as a cruising cutter, 63 ft overall, 53 ft waterline, 13 ft beam and 10 ft 3 in draught. She was later converted to yawl rig and under ownership of Lt. G. Mulhauser R.N.R. sailed around the world during 1920–23, much of the time single-handed.

Her graceful sheer and counter belie the lean, deep sections underwater. She has two jib-topsails set in an unusual fashion to make up for not having a spinnaker. The main shrouds remain set up with deadeyes and lanyards to side channels, to which the bowsprit shroud tackles are set up. The *Amaryllis* was afterwards owned by the Royal Naval College at Dartmouth and used by the cadets for short cruises.

## 71 Primrose IV

The American offshore racing schooner *Primrose IV* beating down the west Solent at the start of the 1926 race round the Fastnet Rock, in which she finished second.

Her owner, Frederick L. Ames, sported a square-sail but her rig was otherwise that of most contemporary small schooner yachts, with a gaff foresail and mainsail proportioned after those of the large north-east American fishing schooners, whose hull form was imitated by many. *Primrose's* well tumbled in quarters, and broad, flat run were typical, as was the absence of lifelines and stanchions.

## 72 Ilex

The Royal Engineer Yacht Club's 50 ft yawl *Ilex* sweeps out past Old Castle Point into Spithead at the start of an offshore race in 1927. The *Ilex* was designed and built at Gosport by Camper and Nicholsons Ltd. as a cruising cutter of 40 ft waterline length, 10 ft 5 in beam and 7 ft 6 in draught. She set 1658 square feet and became a noted competitor in British offshore races during the 1920s, winning the second race round the Fastnet in 1926. The American schooner *Primrose IV* (plate 71) was second, *Saladin* fourth and *Jolie Brise* (plate 68) fifth.

The boat on deck, oilskins and sou'westers are characteristic of offshore racing in the 1920s and 1930s, when a new generation of amateur sailing men took to the sport of passage racing in comparatively small yachts, which had been established in America before 1914 largely by the efforts of Thomas F. Day. The enthusiasts formed the Ocean Racing Club, later the Royal Ocean Racing Club. Although a few of these early offshore racers, such as the Bermudan rigged *Halloween*, carried a full professional crew, the majority were almost totally manned by amateurs, usually with one professional hand, and professional helmsmen were banned.

There was a good deal of work aboard a fifty footer for one man to keep her in racing trim and be expected to do most of the cooking and generally help the rest of the crew, and there was of course no prize money as this was regarded as an unnecessary survival of old traditions which had to be changed. So it was not surprising that professionals generally disliked this new-style offshore racing. However, there were humorous moments. At the end of the stormy Channel race of 1928, after two days and nights of wet windward work, one entry wallowed in towards the finish and, as the gun fired, the Brightlingsea hand turned to the tousled owner and his crew with a grinning 'twice round, Sir'? Seamen who had spent their winters since childhood fishing under sail in the smacks were amused at the pose of some amateurs who assumed participation in passage racing gave them a 'tough' character. But the new style racing flourished and grew to breed a healthy type of yacht and amateur yachtsman, though many of the present designs border on the freakish

**73 Magnet** (*opposite*)

The 51 ft cutter *Magnet* bustles along on a run in 1928, setting a balloon staysail, 'cruising' spinnaker on a very light boom and a curiously arranged yard topsail. She was fresh from her builders, Gilbert and Pascoe of Porthleven, in Mounts Bay, Cornwall, who also designed her, probably influenced by the many pilot cutters built at Porthleven for the Bristol Channel pilots. A healthy beam of 14 ft and draught of 8 ft, the bold bow, ample freeboard, and the boat on deck combine to emphasise the appeal the pilot cutters had to many amateur yachtsmen of the 1920s and 1930s, eager to cruise in all weathers, and to compete in the early English passage races for amateur crews, which grew into the Royal Ocean Racing Club. Nevertheless, the *Magnet* was converted to schooner rig in 1930.

**74 The Norwegian cutter Neptune in a gale, 1928**

The reefed-down cutter *Neptune* bursting along in a gale, 1928. This 60 footer was designed by John Anker and was built at Sogu, Norway, by Abel Marrdrup in 1918; one of the many fine cruising and racing yachts constructed in neutral Norway at that time of prosperity in her shipping trade.

The 49 ft 3 in waterline *Neptune* had 16 ft 3 in beam and drew 10 ft. She set 2628 square feet in a gaff cutter rig. Later she was sold to English owners, having been successively named *Neptune*, and *Albatros*. She competed in the first race around the Fastnet Rock during 1925, which became established as the biennial Fastnet race.

It needed considerable weight of wind to put *Neptune*'s rail down when she was reefed. The mainsail's first reef is neatly taken with a lacing passed through reinforced eyelets in the sail and around its foot (reef lacings or points should *never* be passed around a boom) after the tack and clew pendants were pulled down; a lengthy job. The boom is bending in the strong wind.

Although the short bowsprit has shrouds and spreaders its bobstay is permanently set up with a rigging screw. A light net is spread under it to help the bowspritendman to gather the jib or jib-topsail, when these were sent up or lowered.

These Norwegian craft had exceptionally heavy masts and *Neptune* has a pair of halyard winches mounted on hers, just above the spider band. She was unusual in her day by having stanchions and a guardwire above the low bulwarks.

**75 Bow view of Neptune** (*opposite*)

**76 Merrymaid**

The 98 ft 6 in cruiser-racer ketch *Merrymaid* sails through yachts anchored in Cowes Roads, 1928. *Merrymaid* was another of the fine cruising-style racers produced by designers in the few years before establishment of the International Yacht Racing Union classes in 1906, as a reaction to the lightly built and extreme shaped racing yachts of the Linear Rating rule, which had temporarily stopped construction of first class racing yachts.

The *Merrymaid* was designed and built by Camper and Nicholsons Ltd. in 1904 as a cutter, 68 ft waterline length, 18 ft beam and 13 ft draught. She raced in handicap events and, briefly, with a menagerie big class during the transition to the metre class rule. By 1911 she was re-rigged as a ketch and here sets 4917 square feet in a 1928 handicap race, under the flag of Cecil Slade. For some years she was sailed by Captain Jack Carter of Rowhedge; later resident at Cowes.

**77 Westward and Britannia**

The Bermudan rigged *Britannia* beats down the West Solent ahead of the 323 ton schooner *Westward*

*Westward* was a notable design of Nathaniel G. Herreshoff, built in 1910 at the Herreshoff Manufacturing Company yard at Bristol, Rhode Island, for Alexander Corcoran, who ordered her as a racing schooner fit to beat the German Kaiser's *Meteor IV* The steel hull had little sheer but a well shaped stern. She was 135 ft long overall, 96 ft 1 in waterline, 27 ft 1 in beam and drew 16 ft 11 in. The attractive gaff schooner rig set 15,498 square feet and she carried a crew of 35 hands.

During her first season she won eleven firsts in eleven starts, sailed by the Scotch-American Captain Charles Barr. She was afterwards bought by the Verein Seefahrt of Hamburg, was renamed *Hamburg II* and raced in European waters against similar large schooners.

During 1920 she was fitted out for Clarence ....try, the financier, and in 1924 was sold to ...arwick Brookes, and the following year to ...T. B. Davis, then resident at Guernsey in the ....annel Islands, and commenced many years of ....cing with the large class, of which she was the ....gest yacht.

...Davis was unusual amongst owners of large ....cing yachts in that he not only took her wheel ....ring much of a race but had forceful opinions as ...tactics and racing manoeuvres. Her captain, ...fred Diaper of Itchen, combined diplomacy with ....ne racing record and, although the *Westward* ....quently finished first, she rarely won because of ...r size and consequent handicap. If the course had ....ich reaching, she could romp ahead and perhaps ....e her time but like all schooners she was slower ...windward than the cutters.

...In 1931 her crew made her a new suit of sails ...th its area reduced to 13,455 square feet to obtain

improved racing rating, and in 1934 she won the King's Cup against the big class cutters but the next season was her last, with the full glory of the rivalry of *Britannia*, *Velsheda*, *Endeavour*, *Candida*, *Astra*, and *Shamrock V* matched against her, and all of them against the American sloop *Yankee*, sportingly sailed across to race under Mr. G. B. Lambert.

By 1939 she was reduced to a cruiser with two diesel engines, but retained her majestic rig until she was destroyed in 1948 under the terms of her owner's will which decreed she must be taken into the Channel and sunk–a last duty carried out under the supervision of two of her old racing crew.

She is going well in this photograph, where one can sense the steady, strong breeze, giving this fine racer her best weather but letting the Bermudan cutter rigged *Britannia* eat out to windward in a gradually increasing lead to the next mark.

**78   Westward**

*Westward* becalmed, 4 August 1925. The Yankee jib-topsail is set and a jib is in stops along the bowsprit and led up the forestay, ready to break out when the Yankee is handed. Despite the very light air she is ghosting along with a discernible wake. Some of her crew sit with their legs over the lee side and all hands move quietly and steadily to aid her trim and keep the sails filled. This was yacht schooner rig at its most graceful.

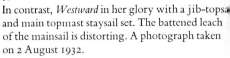

### 80 Shamrock, 23 metre

'*Shamrock, 23 metre*' as the racing yacht fraternity called her, shows off her Marconi topmast in the big class season of 1928.

Although the topsail yard had gone, the jackyard remained and the gaff cutter sail plan had reached its ultimate height in these craft. The mast needed a second set of lower spreaders between the gaff jaws and the deck and these were socketed in after the mainsail was set. She is close on the wind and the lee running and shifting backstay remain set up. A long-roper jib-topsail is set and stands perfectly in creamy, cotton canvas.

In 1908 Sir Thomas Lipton ordered this racing cutter, inevitably to be named *Shamrock*, but she was intended for racing around the coast with the British large class and was not a challenger for the Americas Cup, and therefore had no number in his series of racing yachts.

*Shamrock, 23 metre*, was a long lived and successful racer, at first sailed by Captain Edward Sycamore of Brightlingsea, with a crew from the Colne.

Her class opponents were Miles Kennedy's *White Heather* sailed by Captain Charles Bevis of Bursledon, on the Hamble river, with a predominantly Solent crew; the *Brynhild* skippered by

Captain Steven Barbrook of Tollesbury, Essex, with a crew from there, West Mersea and the river Colne, and the *Nyria* commanded by Captain Steven Ray from Gosport, with a mainly Solent crew. Each yacht had a crew of 22 and set about 10,000 square feet of canvas, without the equally sized spinnaker which set from the topmast head, 120 ft above the deck. Fitted out, these yachts cost £12,000 and a season's racing then cost the owner around £5000.

The *Shamrock* was designed by Fife as a light weather boat and her finest point of sailing was turning to windward in light or moderate breezes. However, they had to take the rough with the smooth in the racing season and in the Nore to Dover race the 23 metres carried whole mainsails through a really heavy sea at the back of the Goodwins, which shook the yachts, straining them from stem to stern as they battled to windward through green seas for three hours, in clouds of spray.

The closeness of racing of these yachts was shown during the 1910 season when after a season of duelling all around the coast, in 40 races, *Shamrock* won 21 first prizes and *White Heather* 19. They sailed without time allowance and usually finished within a boat's length.

In 1911 the *Shamrock* was not fitted out and her crew transferred to the 19 metre *Mariquita* but next year *Shamrock* again raced around the coast with the big class.

During the early 1920s Sir Thomas Lipton had the *Shamrock* fitted out and raced under Captain Leavett of Tollesbury, Essex, then Captain Diaper from Itchen, Hampshire; then again by Captain Sycamore, who had just left the big schooner *Westward*. With some of her old crew back and thoroughly refitted, she enjoyed tremendous sport in a big class including the old *Britannia* skippered by Captain Albert Turner of Wivenhoe, *White Heather* sailed by Captain Ted Mountifield from Gosport, the newer *Lulworth*, last of the big gaff racers to be built, handled by Captain Bevis, and the large schooner *Westward* now sailed by Captain Alf Diaper of Itchen. Later these were joined by new large yachts designed with Bermudan rig; the Fife built *Cambria* and the Nicholson built *Astra* sailed by Captain Pound from Gosport, and in 1929 by the *Candida* with Captain Gilbey of Bosham, with a Chichester harbour crew. In 1930 the *Shamrock* was superseded by the new, Bermudan rigged Americas Cup challenger *Shamrock V* and the old yacht was broken up during 1933.

### 81  Shamrock, 23 metre

The green hulled *Shamrock*, 23 *metre*, running through Cowes Roads in 1928, setting 17,000 square feet in mainsail, staysail, jib, jackyard topsail, baby jib-topsail and spinnaker.

The mainsail foot is stretched on a track along the boom and its head is laced to a rod jackstay on the gaff. The jib-headed topsail is set on a track at the aft side of the topmast of her Marconi rig. It is cut flat with a diagonal seam and the clew is extended by a jackyard which is strengthened by bindings.

The width of the spreaders is worth notice and the battened mainsail leach stands almost perfectly.

The light canvas of the full cut jib hangs limp below, but fills with wind at its head and the baby jib-topsail, set flying, billows out above it, filling the space between the topmast and the spinnaker leach.

The balloon staysail is drawing well but it is the full curve of the creamy-white spinnaker which dominates the photograph; 8000 square feet of power, drawing the *Shamrock* rushing through the Solent.

Captain Edward Sycamore of Brightlingsea, Essex, crouches at the wheel and first mate William Wadley of Rowhedge, a yachting village further up the river Colne, presides over his foredeck in whites; the usual dress of the first mate:

The mate of a large racing yacht had much responsibility. The condition of the yacht's hull, mast spars, rigging and sails were his care at all times, and he was constantly checking it all. In many ways he was harder worked than the captain, from whom he received orders and saw they were carried out as quickly as was humanly possible, and in a racer those words had meaning. His usual racing station was on the foredeck, where he had special charge of the trim of headsails and spinnaker, and of their setting and lowering. On some points of sailing he advised the captain of competitors' tactics, when he had clearer vision forward than the skipper at the helm. In large racers like the *Shamrock*, the second mate had charge of the backstays and mainsheet, and his racing station was aft.

The mate was frequently in charge of the yacht and her navigation at sea, on passage and in harbour. He was amongst the first on deck each morning and the last to turn in to his fo'c'sle cot. In large yachts he was often kept on all winter to superintend or carry out maintenance work.

William Fife, the great Scottish yacht designer who created the *Shamrock* once said at a Clyde Yacht Club dinner that Bill Wadley was 'The best racing mate on the British coast'; a compliment of which he was justly proud.

### 82  White Heather II

The 23 metre racing cutter *White Heather II* running through a crowded Cowes Roads on 7 August 1929, showing the height and grace of the final days of the gaff rigged racers. The auxiliary spreaders half way up the mainsail and topsail luff heights indicate that ingenuity was strained to keep these tall rigs standing. The humming strain in the weather shifting and running backstays can almost be heard.

The staysail and the jib are blanketed by the mainsail, topsail and large spinnaker. The bow-spritendsman and four other hands are sending up a 'long roper' jib-topsail, in stops, others tail on its halyard by the mast and the mate looks anxiously aloft by the lee shrouds. The remainder of the crew and guests gather aft by the captain at her wheel to keep as much movable weight as possible aft while running.

She set 8048 square feet in mainsail, topsail, staysail and jib, but carries almost twice that here with the spinnaker.

'Yachting' as it was done.

### 83 White Heather II

Lord Waring's racing cutter *White Heather II* becalmed on 9 June 1930. The mainsail hangs limp and the light spinnaker puckers as she floats in a glassy calm. Six hands gather aft to keep her stern down and guests chat by the falls of the shifting backstay. The spinnaker boom guy droops and Captain Mountifield of Gosport stands at the wheel frustrated by the calm.

Her fine counter and gentle sheer are typical of the draughting of William Fife. She was built at Fairlie in 1907 and launched from a pontoon in the deeper water off that shallow shore. For many years her captain was Charles Bevis of Bursledon, with a crew mainly from the Solent yachting ports.

### 84 Marken

The 49 ft *Marken* was a steel Dutch boier type yacht built in 1913. She has the Dutch concept of cutter rig for shallow draught craft; under canvassed for light winds, as here, where *Marken* is also motoring in towards Cowes. The boier hull was exceptionally full, excelled only by the Schevenigen Bom or Pink types, but unlike them it was designed for sailing sheltered waters; carrying cargo, or for yachting.

The downhaul from the peak of the gaff is useful in a cruising yacht, when lowering away.

The short gaff span and the single part, wire rope peak halyard leading to a reel winch, are typical, as is the main tack tackle for setting the luff taut after the sail is hoisted by its halyards; a most useful method much used in English small sailing working craft.

### 85 Madcap

The ex-Cardiff pilot skiff *Madcap* surges along to windward in 1938 with a yard rigged for carrying a squaresail when off the wind. This 43 ft 2 in cutter was built by Davies and Plain at Cardiff in 1875 for a Bristol Channel pilot. The beam of 12 ft 3 in and draught of 7 ft 6 in were typical, as was the short, narrow counter, bulwarks and bold bow. When this photograph was taken the *Madcap* had hogged her sheer in way of the chainplates; not unusual in old craft, particularly those like pilot boats, which did not have channels to spread the load of the shrouds because of the occasional need to go alongside ships.

The pole masthead instead of a mast and topmast is probably an alteration for use as a yacht. She was sailed by Rear Admiral F. Burges Watson. A comforting sort of craft when offshore at nightfall with a freshening wind and lump of sea. The fitting of only three mast hoops on the luff of the roller reefing mainsail assists reefing but needs the luff set very taut. The use of moused hook blocks on the peak halyards was typical in many working craft.

## 86 Sunbeam II

The steel, three masted auxiliary schooner *Sunbeam II* was designed by G. L. Watson and Co. and was built by William Denny and Brothers Ltd. in 1929 for shipowner Sir Walter Runciman. This fine 659 tonner is 195 ft overall, 150 ft waterline length, 30 ft 1 in beam and 15 ft 6 in draught. She was built with twin Atlas diesels and was planned as successor to the steam auxiliary, composite three masted schooner *Sunbeam* built for Lord Brassey in 1874, in which he cruised extensively over many seas and oceans, including a voyage around the world.

The original *Sunbeam* was eventually bought by Sir Walter, who liked the type so much that he commissioned the design of the larger, steel schooner which was commissioned as the old *Sunbeam* was sold for breaking up in 1930.

Here *Sunbeam II* stands across the tideway in a

...ght breeze with topmast staysails set. As the star-board side ladder remains rigged, she is not going ...r. The usual complement of boats for a large yacht ...f the period includes a speedboat in davits. The ...arboard boat boom is stowed against the bulwarks. ...he chain bobstay, martingale and spike bowsprit are typical of yachts of this type and the anchors, cat davits, figurehead, bowsprit and general arrangements at the bow are reminiscent of the square rigger age; appropriate for her ownership by a family which had worked its way to riches from seafaring in collier brigs.

The fore staysail, inner and outer jib and a jib-topsail are set. Squaresails could be sent up on the foreyard when wanted. Appropriately, a cargo ship throbs down, astern.

The *Sunbeam II* still sails the seas as the Greek training ship *Eugene Eugenides*.

### 87 Lulworth

*Lulworth* was one of the last of the big racing yachts built with gaff rig. She was designed by Herbert White of White Brothers (Son) Ltd. of Itchen, Hampshire, who built her in 1920 for R. H. Lee. She was launched as the *Terpsichore* but her name changed with ownership to *Lulworth*, in 1924, when she was bought by Herbert Weld, of the noted yachting family who had owned the large racing cutter *Lulworth* in the early 19th century.

*Lulworth*'s 119 ft 6 in overall hull length was shorter than her contemporaries but a beam of 21 ft 10 in and draught of 17 ft 8 in maintained an average displacement. She was a powerful yacht, which seemed slightly old fashioned when built, an atmosphere enhanced by the generous freeboard, low bulwarks (instead of the simple footrail then common) the prominent channels, and the counter timbers. The shape of the bow and counter was also uncompromising but her underwater body was well formed and she often 'got a flag'. Like all large gaff rig racers of the 1920s, her rig was frequently altered and heightened in the search for windward efficiency.

This photograph was taken in August 1929 when she was owned by A. A. Paton, and shows the height of a racing cutter's Marconi topmast and the extensive staying it required. Her topsail had possibly the greatest aspect ratio of any. Windward capability of the rig is shown by the lee running and shifting backstays remaining set up, and she moves well in the light breeze. At that time she was sailed by Scottish captain Archie Hogarth, from Port Bannatyne, Bute, with a crew from the Solent, the Clyde and Essex. During a race in 1930, when the *Lulworth* was running through the Solent, she accidentally ran down and sank the 12 metre *Lucilla*, drowning the steward.

In 1935 the *Lulworth* was converted to a cruising ketch and a diesel engine was installed two years later. She is still in use as a houseboat on the Hamble river.

### 88 Diligent

The ex-Brixham smack *Diligent* fetches into Cowes Roads in a fresh south-westerly during 1936. She was earlier named *Mary Eddy Vane* and was built in 1926 by Sanders and Co. at Galmpton, on the river Dart.

Her hull dimensions of 75 ft overall, 62 ft 6 in waterline length, 18 ft 3 in beam and 9 ft 6 in draught are typical. She set 2545 square feet.

During the 1920s and early '30s dozens of these fine ketches, most only a few years old, were offered for sale at Brixham at very low prices. Trawling under sail flourished in the West Country during and immediately after the 1914–18 war but soon declined, because of growing use of motor driven craft and then economic depression. Many fine smacks such as the *Restless* were bought by yachtsmen and, with holds altered to accommodation, converted to seagoing cruisers; heavy to work but giving pride of ownership and providing some employment for Brixham seafarers as skippers and hands.

At first, Brixham smacks were cutter rigged, then locally known as 'sloops', but as size increased a small 'dandy' mizzen was added and then the ketch rig was adopted, culminating in powerful craft like the *Restless*.

West Country sail plans were generally much lower than elsewhere and the centre of area of the four lowers follows this, the mizzen being particularly short luffed and having a long gaff. A yard topsail could be set above it for light weather passagemaking.

Traditionally Brixham smacks did not carry a bobstay but one has been fitted to the *Diligent* to restrict movement of the long bowsprit and keep the jib luff taut on the wind.

A handsome cruiser, heavy to work and in contrast to the Bermudan sloop lying inshore.

### 90 Altair

The 107 ft 10 in schooner *Altair* slices past Cowes Green on 1 August 1933 in a spanking, reaching breeze.

The *Altair* was designed by W. and R. B. Fife and was launched from W. Fife and Son's yard in 1931; a late but fine example of a large auxiliary cruising schooner built with gaff rig. She is here using all her 77 ft 11 in waterline length. Beam wa 20 ft 6 in and draught 13 ft 2 in.

The *Altair* is setting 5938 square feet in this photograph.

There was a limited revival of racing by large cruising schooners in the 1930s and though of fair heavy displacement they gave good sport on inshore courses.

## 89 Xarifa

The American three masted schooner yacht *Xarifa* gets under way to stretch her new sails which spread 7786 square feet of canvas. The 280 ton *Xarifa* was built by John Samuel White and Co. at Cowes for Mr. F. M. Singer of New York.

She was a deceptively large yacht, 142 ft overall, 100 ft waterline length, 28 ft 2 in beam and 15 ft draught. An auxiliary diesel engine was installed.

Somehow her rig does not seem to quite suit the full-bowed hull, with its generous freeboard and bulwarks, which is surprising as she was designed by J. M. Soper and Son, who draughted some notably good looking yachts.

Her gaff sails retain the vertical cloths traditional in cruising yachts. The topping lifts are arranged, American fashion, with a standing pendant from the masthead ending in a block through which a lift was rove, the forward end made fast to the boom and the other leading through a block at the boom end, then forward along the boom, where it was set up by a purchase.

This cruising schooner of the 1920s makes interesting comparison with Plate 6.

## 91 Elk

Lord Glentanar's powerful cruising schooner *Elk* prepares to race in the large handicap class. The main, foresail, staysail, jib, main jackyard topsail and jib topsail have been set, and hands amidships are preparing to send up the fore topsail.

The *Elk* was designed by G. L. Watson and Co. and was built by Scott's Shipbuilding and Engineering Co. at Greenock in 1928. She was 131 ft 5 in overall, 100 ft waterline, 24 ft 6 in beam and 14 ft draught.

The Bermudan rigged racer fetching across under foresail is thought to be the 'J' class *Velsheda*, owned by W. L. Stephenson and sailed by Captain Mountifield of Gosport, whose crew are preparing to set the mainsail.

### 92 Golden Hind

Captain J. B. Kitson's schooner *Golden Hind* battles it out with a yawl in a cruiser handicap race of the mid 1930s.

This 104 ft 9 in overall schooner was designed by Alfred Mylne and Co. and was 72 ft waterline length, 20 ft beam, 12 ft draught and set 4200 square feet in this rig.

She was built in 1931 by Alexander Stephen and Sons Ltd, the Clyde shipbuilders, in that time of grave depression when even a sizeable shipbuilding yard accepted orders for such a small craft and made a fine job of her composite construction.

The large deckhouse mars her otherwise clean appearance but she is at maximum speed in this picture.

## 93 Rose

The Royal Artillery Yacht Club yawl *Rose* at the start of the Fastnet race, chasing a large Bermudan ketch. The 32 ton *Rose* was designed by J. M. Soper and was built at Southampton by J. G. Fay and Co. in 1899. Soper was designer of the big cutter *Satanita* (plates 1, 2, 13 and 14) and several other large sailing, steam and motor yachts.

The reaching jib is pulling boldly against the taut shifting backstay supporting the topmast head.

The Gunners, as they were known in the contemporary sailing world, seemed to enjoy the *Rose*, before passing on to a more modern yacht. She was still sailing in the 1960s.

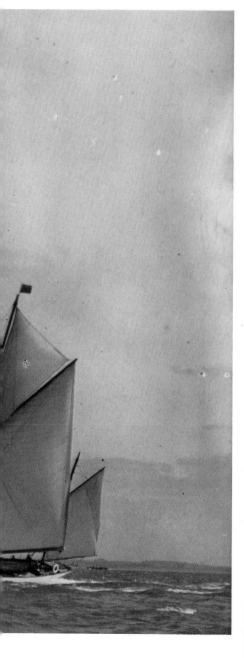

## 94 Dyarchy

The ex-Bristol Channel pilot skiff *Dyarchy* thrashing through the Solent in a fresh breeze under jib and mainsail, with her owner, Roger Pinckney, at the helm, 1931.

Scores of similar, cutter rigged 'skiffs' were built and owned from the Bristol Channel ports of Bristol, Cardiff, Newport, Barry, and especially from the small village of Pill, on a creek off the Avon river, below Bristol. Most had a short counter or lute stern but others, including *Dyarchy*, had a transom. These boats achieved a reputation amongst yachtsmen for seaworthiness, probably founded on the modest sail area and the seamanship of their crews.

When steam cutters were introduced to the Bristol Channel service after the 1914–18 war, the sailing skiffs were rapidly sold off. Many were bought by yachtsmen, as little conversion work was needed, and some are still sailing.

The 41 ft *Dyarchy* was built at Pill in 1901 by Cooper, a noted builder of the type, which was usually designed by the making of a half model from which the offsets were taken and the frames made; a system which sometimes resulted in unfair or crudely formed craft with a tendency to lean bows and deep, U-shaped sections. *Dyarchy's* beam was 12 ft 9 in and draught 7 ft. The mast stepped well aft, reducing the length of the boom, which in many was fitted for roller reefing to suit short-handed working, but the gaffs were long, as in *Dyarchy* and bent in strong winds. She has a pole masthead, but many skiffs often carried a topmast. The large staysail, stowed in this photograph, gave power off the wind and the well cut jib did most of the windward work and is set smart with a taut luff.

The crane supporting the throat halyard was of unusual U-shaped design. The spinnaker boom is topped up the mast but these cutters were generally dull sailers in light airs, despite a total working sail area of about 1200 square feet.

Pilot skiffs were notably dry on deck and the comparatively deep bulwarks, small steering cockpit and substantial hatches and skylight over the saloon added to the feeling of security in bad weather.

The tumbled-in quarters and iron tiller are interesting features.

Annual races for the skiffs were held at many Bristol Channel ports but other than in competition amongst themselves, these cutters were slow but seaworthy craft, built to stand hard weather hove-to and to be sailed home by one hand, if necessary, after the pilot owners were boarded to inward bound ships, or seaward to take them off outward bounders.

In 1937 the *Dyarchy* was replaced by a new, larger, cutter yacht designed by J. Laurent Giles of Lymington, who produced one of the finest examples of a modern gaff rigged craft for Roger Pinckney.

## Gwenaloe

[Th]e cutter yacht *Gwenaloe* beats to windward on a
[su]n sparkled sea. Her boxy, tucked up counter,
[flu]sh deck, bulwarks and skylight over the saloon
[ar]e typical of cruisers of the 1880s.

The shifting backstay from the topmast head is
[se]t up to the weather quarter and the lee shifter
[han]gs slack under the belly of the mainsail. The lee
[run]ning backstay has been taken forward to the
[sh]rouds. The bobstay has been well set up, steeving
[th]e moderate length bowsprit downwards and
[en]abling the jib and jib-topsail to set with taut luffs
[in] this sheltered water. Trimming a jib-topsail re-
[qu]ires patience and skill in light airs and strength
[an]d nerve in strong winds, when the shifting back-
[sta]y must be set up before sheeting this sail, well
[na]med 'the topmast breaker'.

A roller reefing mainsail and well setting jib-
[he]aded topsail complete the rig of this well found
[cru]iser.

The 32 ton *Gwenaloe* is competing in the 1934
[Co]wes to Dinard race.

### 98 Bluenose

*Bluenose*, the 142 ft Canadian fishing schooner, fetches slowly across the Solent in light airs durin her visit to Britain in 1935 to attend the Jubilee Naval review of King George V. She sets the rig' gaff mainsail and foresail, a boomed staysail, jib, jib-topsail, fore gaff topsail and main gaff topsail with a 'fisherman's staysail' between the masts. T generous freeboard of her black hull is set off by swinging sheerline but the knuckled bow was th result of incorrect laying-off before building commenced, and remained a distinguishing feature.

*Bluenose* was the first fisherman by Canada's noted yacht designer W. J. Roue, built at Lunenberg by Smith and Rhuland. She was intended primarily to regain the Dennis Cup and also to b competitive as a salt banker, making two trips ea year line-fishing with dories, besides a winter voyage to the West Indies with salt cod cargo, returning with salt from Turks Island. She displace 285 tons and could load 210 tons of cargo.

The *Bluenose* was 111 ft 9 in waterline length, 27 ft beam and 15 ft 8 in draught; typical dimensic of these fishing schooners of north-east Canada and America. Throughout her long fishing career

**96  Manou** *(opposite)*

The French topsail schooner yacht *Manou* motor-sailing off Cowes. This wooden 106 footer was designed and built by E. Bonne at Paimpol, a little schooner-building port on the gulf of St. Malo. She was launched in 1912 as the *Araok* and with 24 ft 7 in beam and 9 ft 10 in draught the hull was typical of the many fishing and cargo-carrying schooners built there until the 1920s. Shapely, hard working little ships in the line-fishing, and coasting and short sea trades. By 1930 she was a yacht, owned by Georges Bourgeois and registered at Le Havre.

The *Manou* set 2538 square feet of plain sail and had two Kelvin petrol engines installed as auxiliaries.

The gaff foresail has four brails and its loose foot enabled it to be brailed to the mast when reefing or bringing up. The square topsail has roller reefing on the upper yard, which carries a rotating yard below around which the topsail furled when the reefing lines were hauled from the deck, saving going aloft, so long as the gear worked properly.

The standing bowsprit has stout bobstays and a net slung below it for safety when the crew were handling the jibs.

She was sailed by Captain Angus Walters with a full crew of 28.

The topsail luffs set on hoops to the topmasts. A large jib is stopped along the bowsprit which carries plenty of sail stops and has a net slung below it. The working sail area of 10,970 square feet compares with the 10–14,000 set by a large gaff-rigged racing cutters and schooners.

These schooners were from a totally different tradition to British fishing craft, which generally had to be capable of beating to windward in steep seas and tidal waters.

The north-eastern American schooners were fast on a reach or off the wind but were comparatively slow performers dead to windward. When the *Bluenose* was built, most comparable American fishing schooners had auxiliary motors installed and had been designed for auxiliary power for two decades. In Canada things moved more slowly and the *Bluenose* remained engineless until the 1940s, at the end of her fishing career.

**97  German wishbone ketch**

Wishbone was a controversial rig during the 1920s and 1930s in America, Germany and Britain as a combination of gaff and bermudan rig with many of the faults of both.

The divided wishbone gaff was the principal feature of the rig, which was usually applied to ketches, but also to a few three-masted 'schooners', which had a small mizzen.

The intention was to retain useful sail area aloft, similar to the peak of a gaff sail, while trimming the sail to stand flatter to windward by a wire vang led from the gaff end to a swivel block at the mizzen-mast head. This vang was the rig's weakest feature; if it broke in strong winds the gaff and mainsail would probably get out of control and be destroyed, possibly also damaging the mainmast. At best it was subject to constant chafe when the sail was set, and needed frequent renewal as the 'nip' came in the same place at each setting.

The rig was also intended to ease sail handling in small seagoing yachts (important to the amateur crews then increasingly taking to racing offshore), by dividing the sail area among more readily managed sails and reducing reefing to the dousing of sails in an order, to preserve balance. Generally the rig was successful for cruising but too divided for speed in offshore racing, though notable yachts such as the American *Vamarie* were exceptions.

Here a German wishbone ketch reaches along, showing the lee side of the wishbone staysail taking the curve of the divided gaff with its trimming vang.

She sets foresail, wishbone staysail, mizzen stay-sail and mizzen. The single headsail has a boomed foot which does not seem to affect its set.

The graceful hull, curved cockpit coamings, capstan and main hatch have an old fashioned appearance typical of Abeking and Rasmussen designs of that period, though most were fast boats. She flies the ensign of Nazi Germany in the weather shrouds.

*Bluenose* at anchor, showing her unusual, knuckled stem profile, spike bowsprit and staysail boom. The detail of the standing and running rigging is worth study, and the length of the mainboom of these schooners is well shown. The large mainsail was lowered and replaced by a trysail in bad weather, and particularly when the schooner's many line-fishing dories were afloat, scattered on the heaving seas around the mother ship with one or two men in each, line-fishing for cod or haddock. The 14/15 ft, flat bottomed, open dories were stowed inside each other in small stacks, between the fore and main masts, and were hoisted in and out by masthead tackles. When these were all fishing, only the captain and the cook remained on board to watch over them and sail the schooner to recover them.

With the catch pitched on board and the dories hoisted in, the crew began cleaning, salting and stowing the fish in the hold. It was a hard trade in which many were drowned in the frail dories on the fishing banks; a life accurately captured by Rudyard Kipling in his *Captain's Courageous*.

## 99 Bluenose

This is a characteristic shot which shows *Bluenose* to advantage and emphasises the well-sheered, sea-worthy ends. Many similar fishing schooners were owned and sailed from Halifax and Lunenberg. During 1920 local fishing interests and a newspaper proprietor originated a challenge cup for competition between American and Canadian fishing schooners, with Gloucester, Massachusetts being the rivals. These events caused much controversy and in 1921 *Bluenose* was built, partially to race for this trophy.

To meet her, Gloucester fishermen and yachts-men sent the 119 ft *Elsie*, when their new 143 ft *Mayflower* was refused entry as a 'yacht'. In 1922 *Bluenose* met and defeated the Gloucester schooner *Henry Ford*, touching 13 knots in one race, and next year beat the schooners *Shamrock* and *Elizabeth Howard* in Gloucester's Centennial race. Later that year *Bluenose* beat the Gloucester *Columbia* in one race but lost the second on protest, and withdrew.

In 1930 *Bluenose* was challenged by the *Gertrude L. Thebaud*, last of the big North American sailing fishermen, to a private match off Gloucester. The *Bluenose* lost, as she came ill-prepared from fishing, but in 1931, the last race for the Cup, *Bluenose* beat the *Thebaud* in all three races. The rivals met for the last time in 1938 when the match was again marred by disputes. Each won two races and *Bluenose* the final one. She became a Canadian legend and represented Canada's fishing fleet at the 1935 Jubilee Naval Review of King George V in Spithead.

*Bluenose* took a pounding attempting to sail home. Later she was sold to the West Indies for trading and was lost off Haiti in 1946.

In 1963 a replica schooner, *Bluenose II* was sponsored by a Halifax brewery and was built to the same design, in the same yard, and had her trial sail with her original designer and captain on board. The *Bluenose II* remains in use as a reminder of the fine fishing schooners.

### 101 Our Lizzie

The auxiliary ketch *Our Lizzie* was built by W. J. Oliver and Son at Porthleven, on Mounts Bay, Cornwall in 1920 as an auxiliary fishing lugger for St. Ives. During the late 1930s she was converted to a yacht, owned by Mr and Mrs Hugh Bevan. The odd combination of counter stern and slightly tumbled-in bulwarks were common in Cornish drifters of the period and the lean-bowed hull with 6 feet draught and 14 ft 3 in beam carried the low gaff ketch rig well, but was marred by the boxy deckhouse.

These small drifters were a hybrid type following the earlier fast-sailing luggers which had a tall, dipping lug foresail tacked to the stem head and a standing lug mizzen sheeted to a long outrigger. The *Our Lizzie* was originally rigged for fishing with a small lugsail forward and a well steeved gaff mizzen aft, with principal propulsion by a paraffin engine on the centreline and typically, another smaller engine on the starboard quarter as emergency power in case of breakdown and to add something to speed.

The ketch rig, setting topsails, is not pointing very high as she beats down the Solent in a light breeze.

**102 Kismet** (*below*)

The 16 ton *Kismet* was one of the author's favourite cutters when she raced in the handicap classes in the late 1940s. She was designed by W. Fife, Junior, and was built by W. Fife and Son in 1899 as a fast cruiser setting 1390 square feet.

Orson Wright and C. H. Pearse raced her hard before and just after the 1939–45 war, basing *Kismet* at West Mersea, Essex, where she now lies as a houseboat, shorn of mast and spars.

Here she beats to windward off Gurnard in a handicap class on 1 August 1939.

**103 Cachalot** (*above*)

The fine cruising ketch *Cachalot* outward bound for a cruise to the Mediterranean and the Red Sea in 1936.

*Cachalot* was designed and built for Lt.-Col. Claude Beddington by J. W. and A. Upham of Brixham, Devon, generally following the lines and rig of a Brixham trawl smack, but with refined construction and rig. She was 76 ft 7 in overall length, 67 ft 8 in waterline length, 19 ft 2 in beam and 9 ft 10 in draught. Sail area was generous and a Gardner diesel auxiliary was used in calms.

Her owner was a sea fishing enthusiast and with a Brixham skipper and crew, enjoyed some notable cruising and occasionally sportingly entered in large handicap class races in the Solent.

## 104 Chanticleer

The boier *Chanticleer* motoring in a calm, 1929.

This steel 50 footer was built at Lemmer in 1910 with the narrow strakes of plating typical of contemporary Dutch small craft practice. Most gaff rigged Dutch fishing and coastal craft had relatively narrow gaff mainsails with short, often slightly curved, gaffs, and luffs laced to the mast, as seen here, with hardwood parrel beads or circular rollers on the lacing, to reduce friction.

A staysail (more correctly the stay-foresail, or fore staysail) set to the stemhead or to a short metal bumkin projecting from it, and a jib set on a long running bowsprit, which was not always run out in confined waters. Here the *Chanticleer* is setting a very large, light-weather jib which is temporarily aback across the forestay.

The long, narrow varnished leeboards have a flat outer face but are shaped on the inboard sides to obtain lift to windward. The heavy mast steps in an oak tabernacle which carries the boom gooseneck at its after side; a very practical arrangement with a loose footed sail. *Chanticleer*'s beam of 13 ft 4 in and draught of 3 ft 6 in were typical of these roomy vessels which had a vogue amongst some English cruising owners during the 1920s and '30s, and are still often seen in British waters.

*Chanticleer*'s owner, then probably Mr Knowles Edge, stands by the shrouds while his skipper and a hand carry on preparing for the day's passage.

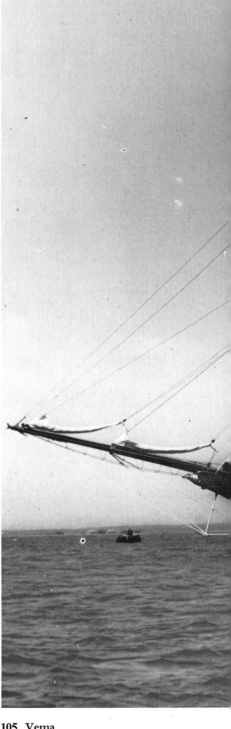

## 105 Vema

The 822 ton, American three-masted schooner *Vema* at anchor, 1938. From her eagle figurehead to the sweeping counter she exhibits the grace and power of the large sailing yacht, though the deckhouses detract from her profile.

The rig is well proportioned and its staying can e traced in detail.

She was built by Burmeister and Wain at openhagen in 1923 to the design of Cox and evens of New York and was launched as the ussar for an American owner. Her hull was 202 ft 6 in overall, 164 ft waterline, 33 ft 2 in beam and 14 ft 7 in draught. Two diesel engines manufactured by the builders gave good speed under power, when she was steered from the navigating bridge by the foremast. A funnel for the auxiliaries is on the port side, forward.

The peak halyards are set up with canvas strops around the stowed and coated gaff sails and the headsails hang, coated and picked-up by their halyards.

A yacht capable of going anywhere she could float.

## 106 Harkaway

The West Solent one-design class boat *Harkaway* sets a racing wishbone rig in 1938. A light wishbone gaff extends a diagonally cut mainsail, with its luff running on a mast track. The gaff end has a peak halyard leading from the masthead to trim its setting angle, and a pair of vangs to assist in reducing twist in the mainsail. The high clewed foresail is interesting. The mast has three sets of spreaders.

*Harkaway*'s owner is at the tiller as she slides past the Royal Yacht Squadron at Cowes and the single hand, then usual in this class, keeps his eye on everything, so his owner has a good day's sport.

The West Solent Restricted class were designed by Rodney Paul of the Berthon Boat Company, who built them around 1927. Dimensions were 34 ft 5 in overall, 24 ft waterline, 7 ft 5 in beam and 5 ft 4 in draught, and sail area 530 square feet, which most of the class set in a bermudan sloop rig. These fine little yachts were principally raced by members of the Royal Lymington Yacht Club. After being renamed *Goosander*, then reverting to *Harkaway*, she is now sailed from Glasson Dock by D. and M. Sheppard.

## 107 Gaff-rig race

Resembling an old photograph of a fleet of Polperro line fishers setting out for the grounds, or the Colne Oyster fishery in the days of sail, this shot of part of a fleet at the annual Solent gaff rig race shows the variety of small craft entering in these events, which have attracted growing numbers of entries since the first was held on the Essex coast in 1962.

In Britain, gaff rig races are now held on the east, south-west and north-east coasts, and on the Solent and the Clyde, and similar events are organised in America for types such as the Muscongus Bay or Friendship sloops and for catboats, bringing together craft and owners for friendly competition, rounded off with a dinner and joyful prizegiving.

## 08  Dreva

The Cornish cutter yacht *Dreva* was built in 1936 by W. Frazier and Son of Mevagissey as the *Happy Return*. Her bold bow and sheer, and tumbled-in quarters mark her as a design by Nigel Warington Smyth, one of a family of Cornish yachtsmen and designers of small craft who have enriched the small boat world with many delightful craft, power and sail.

*Dreva* is 34 ft 1 in overall, 30 ft waterline length, 9 ft beam and 6 ft draught. She carries 737 square feet and here sets a large reaching jib from the end of her well steeved bowsprit.

The mainsail has roller reefing and a row of reef points in the storm reef position. Vangs are rigged from the gaff end to reduce twist in the mainsail, unusual practice in British gaff-rigged yachts.

The large deckhouse interrupts the helmsman's vision but enlarges the accommodation in the usually congested entrance to the saloon from the cockpit.

This is a cruising yacht of classic concept.

## 109  Marishka

The cutter *Marishka* roars along under a yard topsail and reaching jib, with the ex-Brixham smack *Vigilance* coming up astern.

The *Marishka* was designed by D. Fyfe and was built by Moris and Lorimer at Sandbank, on the Clyde, in 1895. She is 27 ft 6 in overall, 25 ft waterline length, 8 ft 6 in beam and 5 ft 6 in draught.

She sets 390 square feet in cutter rig and has a staysail boom pivoted at the deck; a feature frequently seen in American yachts, which trims the staysail clew to its optimum for windward sailing at each tack, often rigged with a 'lazy' sheet which does not need tending when going about; useful when short-handed. However, its set can only be varied by going forward and slackening or tautening the clew lacing to the boom end, and it is often an embarrassment on a busy foredeck, though it does spread the staysail efficiently when running.

A strong permanent boom gallows is a desirable feature in a yacht used for offshore sailing as the boom can be lowered on it and lashed down while the mainsail is reefed; avoiding those dangerous, uneasy lurches while the pendants are settled and the points tied in a seaway. Although traditionally unacceptable, the gallows also provides useful handholds aft but can be dangerous if the mainsheet fouls it. Like the *Sumurun*, racing in the same waters many years earlier (plate 60), the *Marishka* has a second racing flag at the top of her topsail yard.

## 110  Plover

The gaff ketch *Plover* was designed and built by David Hillyard, at Littlehampton, in 1932, as one of his series of standard cruising yachts, which have attracted cruising yachtsmen since he established his yard there after leaving his native river Colne. Dan Webb was another of his contemporaries at the Rowhedge yards, who also set up his own business, at Maldon, building the Blackwater Sloops as small standard cruisers.

David Hillyard believed in giving value for money, and in producing a sound, plainly finished craft at a price many could afford. He maintained this policy with many types of standard wooden yachts, which are still built by the firm.

The 30 ft *Plover* was launched in 1932; 26 ft waterline length, 9 ft beam and 4 ft draught. She sets 500 square feet. The gaff ketch, with a gaff mizzen, is not a weatherly rig but the *Plover* seems to be standing to windward well and there is no doubt of its usefulness when seagoing in stronger winds. Her main boom looks slender for the sail area and the mainmast has narrow spreaders.

Pointed-stern yachts had a vogue amongst cruising yachtsmen between about 1905–55 and there is an occasional revival by devotees of the fishing, pilot and life-saving craft, and yachts, by the Norwegian designer Colin Archer.

## 111 Vigilance

The 39 ton *Vigilance* was built by J. W. and A. Upham of Brixham in 1926, the last such smack built by the firm.

She is surging along on a reach with the big foresail set, often referred to as a 'tow foresail' by the crews, from its use to maintain speed over the ground when trawling. A well-proportioned jib and jib-topsail compliment her sail spread. The topmast is sprung forward in jaunty fashion. The mainmast is stepped well aft, a feature of many Brixham and Plymouth fishing ketches.

A suit of working sails for these smacks included mainsail and topsail, mizzen and topsail, stay foresail, big foresail, mizzen staysail and four jibs of various sizes from large to storm.

The Brixham smacks were developed to trawl grounds in the western part of the English Channel and later also worked in the Bristol Channel and Irish Sea. Some Brixham smacks also worked in the trawl fishery off Dover and Hastings; later extending their ventures to work from Ramsgate, Lowestoft, Great Yarmouth and Scarborough, coming into competition with the trawling fleets from Barking, the Colne and elsewhere. As railways spread to the east coast ports, offering quick carriage for fish to industrial markets, the Brixham smacks joined with scores of others from Barking and north-east Essex to use and develop them, and the concentrated trawling of the North Sea from the developed ports of Grimsby, Hull, Lowestoft and Yarmouth began. By the 1880s Brixham smacks began to desert the North Sea to fish the Bristol Channel and Irish Sea grounds, and this and Channel trawling became their mainstay.

By 1914 over 300 trawlers worked from Brixham but many were lost in the war and ten years later only 80 remained, of which a handful survived into the 1930s, and a very few still sail as yachts. By the time the *Vigilance* and her sisters were built they fished mainly between Portland and the Scillies.

When built, a smack like the *Vigilance* cost £2500 ready for sea and few could risk that amount, afford the maintenance or find adequate crew.

**12 Vigilance**

lift of the headsails; the lee side of the Brixham ketch *Vigilance*, bustling along with jib topsail set above the jib and a big foresail. The generous freeboard and deep bulwarks are typical of the Brixham smack type but the large deckhouse, side ports jib topsail and wheel steering are additions for yacht use.

The long chainplates carried up the bulwarks to the lower deadeyes of the lanyards setting up the shrouds were typical of fishing smacks of this size from many British ports. It was an arrangement vulnerable to damage to the bulwarks from big seas or when streaming or boarding a trawl, and the use of strong channels spreading the inward load of the chainplates across several frames would

have been better, but was thought to interfere with trawl gear.

The large amateur crew are out for a day's enjoyment, but before 1914 a smack like *Vigilance* carried four hands, including one or two boys. This small crew was only possible with the adoption of the steam capstan, which replaced at least two hands. The capstan was mounted just abaft the mainmast and by fairleads and snatch blocks almost every rope in the smack could be led to it and its power could set the mainsail, get the trawl in and out, hoist the boat aboard, run the bowsprit in and out and sheet the sails in a breeze.

**113  Little Apple**

The three-quarter decked cutter *Little Apple* sports

a well set jackyard topsail set on the pole masthead and an ample mainsail, which prudently has five rows of reef points for stronger winds. She was built at St. Ives, Cornwall, in 1911 for a fisherman who was also keen on occasionally racing her in regattas, and is believed to have worked at one time on the River Fal oyster fishery under the name *White Heather*.

Similar small cutters with large cockpits are still used to dredge those grounds under sail, though most have auxiliary engines, a tradition perpetuated for conservation of the fishery which could, economically, be worked efficiently by a couple of motor craft.

She is now owned by P. Boyce of Wyke Regis, Dorset, and is a fast and weatherly craft.

## 114 Little Apple

The view many competitors in gaff rig races get of *Little Apple*'s narrow, West Country transom. Her large cockpit is ideal for day sailing and racing and here she is going well to windward, the foresail luff a little slack and the boom bending in the freshening breeze. The scroll ending of the cove line at the wale is a nice touch. Her mast is, unusually, stepped at the forward coaming, rather than through the foredeck.

## 115 America

A near replica of the schooner yacht *America* of 1851 sweeps through the Solent in 1973, captured by Roger Smith's camera.

The original *America* was built in 1851 for a syndicate of New York Yacht Club members to represent the American nation in English waters during that year of the International Exhibition. George Steers designed the rakish 100-footer, modelling her after his speedy New York pilot boats, and the excellent proportions of hull and well setting sails contributed largely to her success. She was 80 ft long on the keel, 23 ft beam, and drew 11 ft.

After the transatlantic passage to Cowes she found English yachtsmen welcoming but, at first, unwilling to race. However, eventually a race was arranged over the Royal Yacht Squadron course round the Isle of Wight for a £100 cup presented by the Squadron. The *America* started, without handicap, against seventeen English yachts ranging from the 393 ton schooner *Brilliant* to the little 47 ton cutter *Aurora*, and including such fliers as *Alarm* and the sleek cutter *Volante*, fresh from John Harvey's Wivenhoe yard, manned by a Colneside crew under Captain George Pittuck, and England's pride *Volante* and other leading yachts rounded the Nab Light as was customary and stated in the sailing directions, but the race programme made no mention of it and the *America*, accompanied by several English yachts, stood inshore and to windward emerging with a clear lead. In turning to windward along the island's south shore, *America* was overhauled by the leading English yachts until *Arrow* got ashore and *Alarm* stood by to assist. Shortly afterwards the crack *Volante* was fouled by *Freak* and lost her bowsprit, leaving the *America* to win by eight minutes from the *Aurora*.

Although protested for not rounding the Nab, *America* was awarded the Cup and after winning a match against the small schooner *Titania*, was sold to an English owner. The Cup she had won was eventually presented by her owners to the New York Yacht Club as a trophy for international competition. Interest in it lagged until Mr Ashbury, a member of the Royal Harwich Yacht Club, challenged for it in 1870. His 188 ton schooner *Cambria* beat the American *Dauntless* in a race across the Atlantic, only to lose the Cup Race, held on what was to become its traditional course off the approaches to New York.

Subsequently many challengers from several countries have attempted, unsuccessfully, to regain the Americas Cup, which since 1958 has been raced for by yachts of the 12 metre class.

The replica *America* was designed from the various surviving lines plans said to be constructed from offsets lifted from the hull of the original, after she was sold to English owners in 1851. Her rig was altered to a staysail and jib, instead of the single large jib set by the *America* in 1851, which was sheeted with tackles. The gaff foresail was fitted with a boom whereas the original was a boomless 'lug sheet' foresail, with the clew reaching abaft the main shrouds.

The broad, well rounded quarters and low freeboard are accurately reproduced but the differences and additions, such as a radar scanner aloft and larger deckhouses, detract from her appearance, and an auxiliary diesel engine was installed. Nevertheless, she makes a notable yacht, with a fine turn of speed and was sailing from the Solent during 1973–74, before returning to America.

**116  La Goleta**

he Alden-designed schooner *La Goleta* lends a hint
old-time glory to a 1976 gaff rig race. The gaff
resail enables her to be included in this book and
this race, though the bermudan mainsail
barred her from the prize list.

  She was built by W. J. Yarwood and Son Ltd at
orthwich, Cheshire, whose usual work was steel
gs, barges and small motor coasters. However,
ey made a good job of this schooner which is
ft 6 in waterline, 12 ft 8 in beam and 7 ft 4 in
aught. She sets 1820 square feet.

**117  Shamrock (smack)**

o mistaking this stern as an Essex smack. The
ft *Shamrock* was designed and built by Robert
dous at Brightlingsea in 1900. She was named
er the racing cutter *Shamrock* which challenged
r the Americas Cup in 1899. These shapely
unters were difficult to construct but enabled
ese cutters to work a good sized trawl beam
handle up to four shellfish dredges on
ch side.

  Roger Smith's camera has exactly caught the
btle curves and tumble-in of the quarters. The
ar on the boom is typical; the eye of the topping
t slips over a shoulder at the boom end. The first
ef pendant is rove and others are ready at the
e boom end. The clew outhaul of the loose footed
ainsail is well set up and the mainsheet arrange-
nt remains as it was when she was fishing.
owever, the luff lacing is an alteration from the
ditional mast hoops, which allow the tack to be
ced up to reduce the mainsail area.

  Although registered at Colchester, at the
vigable head of the river Colne, these cutters
re never owned there but were owned in
nsiderable numbers at the villages and small
wns of Rowhedge, Wivenhoe and Brightlingsea
the Colne and at West Mersea, Tollesbury,
adwell and Maldon on the adjoining river
ackwater.

**118  Shamrock (smack)**

The smack *Shamrock* gybing. She is 44 ft overall
and 37 ft waterline length.

  The hull and rig are typical but the large
coachroof is an addition for converting the fish
hold to accommodation.

  The *Shamrock* sank during the icy winter of 1962
but was raised and eventually refitted and re-rigged
by Bryan Thomas of Colchester for pleasure
sailing. In 1974 she was sold to A. Janes of Ottery
St. Mary, Devon and sails from the river Exe.

  Essex smacks of this size, around 15–18 tons,
were the most numerous type and were principally
built between 1875 and 1900, for spratting with the
stow net, fish trawling, dredging oysters, mussels
and 'five fingers' (starfish) and for salvaging – as
giving assistance to wrecked or stranded vessels or
salvaging their cargo, gear and equipment from
them was locally termed.

  The Essex smacksmen saved thousands of
distressed seafarers in this way, usually in winter
and often in appalling conditions of bad weather
and amongst the intricate shoals of that coast.

  Smaller smacks, which often did not carry
a topmast, were used to dredge oysters and trawl
in the rivers and estuaries of the Colne, Blackwater, Crouch and Roach. Larger cutters and
ketches, from 55–80 ft long, were also owned,
principally from the Colne, and fished for sprats
and dredged deep-sea oysters and scallops on many
grounds off the British, Dutch and French coasts,
the North Sea and the English Channel. These bold
vessels were also much used for salvaging and their
speed led many to be chartered to carry fish from
the North Sea fishing fleets to market, and some
carried salmon on the Irish and Scottish west coasts
and lobsters from Norway to England.

  The men who owned and sailed the Essex
smacks were amongst the world's finest fore and
aft sailors and many spent their summers as captains
and crew of racing yachts until 1939.

### 119 Catriona

*Catriona* bounds along under a gaff ketch rig which seems to suit her raised-deck hull, which has an appearance suggestive of a motor cruiser, with similar advantage in spacious accommodation.

She was built by William Osborne of Littlehampton in 1922 and was refitted by M. Taplin, her present owner, in 1972, after lying unused at Portsmouth.

The low sail plan, with its area extended at each end, is well suited to a long keeled, shoal draught hull, and provides flexibility in use as main propulsion or for steadying or auxiliary canvas when motoring. The three reefs in her mainsail suggest she sometimes sails in hard conditions.

In the background the 37ft cutter *Rhoda Gostelow*, built by A. Gostelow at Boston, Lincolnshire in 1937 as the yacht *Northseaman*, also beats to windward. With a waterline length of 30ft 4in, 11 ft 1 in beam and 5 ft 6in draught, she is similar to the small cutter smacks which fished in The Wash, trawling flatfish and dredging shellfish.

### 120 Nellie

The fishing cutter *Nellie* beats to windward 113 years after her launch from Dan Hatcher's Belvedere yard in Northam, Southampton, with Mr Banks, grandson of one of her earlier owners, at the tiller.

The 21 ft 9in *Nellie* was typical of the style of Solent fishing cutters of the mid 19th century and was built about 1863 for trawling fish and dredging oysters in Southampton Water, the West Solent and Spithead, owned by a Mr Giles of Itchen Ferry, who later moved to Cowes. About 1878 she was bought, in dilapidated condition, by a Captain Banks of Hythe and was repaired by Charles Payne at his yachtyard at West Quay, Southampton. During 1886 she was at Rye, Sussex, where fire severely damaged her bow and she was reconditioned and lengthened about 1 ft 8in forward by H. Luke at Itchen Ferry.

In those days she carried the then usual boomless gaff mainsail or 'sheet mainsail' as it was known and had a very long bowsprit. A boom was only

fitted about 1922, when a longer mast was stepped. After 1908 she was mainly used for pleasure sailing by the Banks family but occasionally fished.

The shapely, full bodied *Nellie* has 7 ft 10 in beam and only draws 2 ft 9 in but, like most Solent fishing cutters, goes to windward moderately well and is fast on a reach.

Here her white canvas and yard topsail are a reminder of the old style Solent area regattas which, like those of their contemporaries in Essex were hard fought sailing matches between professionals out to get the utmost out of their fishing craft.

The *Nellie* is, perhaps the closest of surviving Solent fishing cutters to her original concept and arrangement.

## 121 Fanny

The ex-Cowes fishing cutter *Fanny* fetching into Cowes with a heavily reefed mainsail before a squally south-west wind, promising a harder blow.

When this photograph was taken the *Fanny* had been re-rigged with a high-peaked mainsail and increased height of jib halyard. If necessary, the mainsail can be snugged right down with a balance reef just below the throat.

The staysail tack shackles to a short iron bumkin projecting from the stemhead. The length of bowsprit was typical of the Solent fishing cutters, which tended to be hard on the helm in strong winds and usually carried a specially long tiller for those conditions. The boat was built with an open well aft of the mast, having the types usual fish tray or trawl deck sunk below the sheer aft.

Although the Solent fishing boats drew little water, they were a fast and weatherly type which converted readily for pleasure use. Many were built of good timber and workmanship by yacht-yards, and others by shipwrights in their spare time, including the *Fanny*.

The 22 ft × 8 ft 4 in *Fanny* was built by John Watts for Edmund Paskins and fished for oysters, prawns and bottom fish with dredges and trawls until 1937, when she was sold to become a pleasure craft.

Like most of the Solent fishing boat type the *Fanny* has the staysail set to a short iron bumkin, stayed to the stem at the waterline. The reef in this sail saves shifting it for a smaller in strong winds.

Under ownership of the Cook family of Ipswich, Suffolk, the *Fanny* has a good record of racing in gaff rig events on the east coast of England and in the Solent.

The cabin top, cockpit, mainsheet horse, stanchions and guardwire are not original.

### 123 Black Bess

The ex-Solent fishing cutter *Black Bess* sails in company with a clinker-built cutter. The *Black Be[ss]* is believed to have been built about 1870 at Portsmouth for local trawling and dredging.

Her dimensions are 18 ft 3 in, 6 ft 9 in beam and 3 ft 3 in draught. In later years she was bought by the Chatfield family of Wootton who kept her at Fishbourne, Isle of Wight, fishing with her throu[gh] three generations, until she was sold in 1974. She [is] now owned by N. Gaches who occasionally tows a trawl with her in Spithead.

The clinker cutter has an unusual upswept counter and sets a small yard topsail. Her sideligh[ts] are carried at a sensible height on the shrouds.

### 122 Brunette

The 21 ft 9 in cutter *Brunette* is believed to have been built at Cowes in 1924, possibly as a gentleman's afternoon sailing boat, which also towed a trawl occasionally for fun, as she had a fish deck aft in the manner of local fishing craft.

After being bermudan rigged and having a coach roof added she was cruised and raced for some years before being restored and re-rigged in 1976 by her present owner, Chris Waddington. She sets the staysail to the stemhead and has points for two deep reefs in the loose footed mainsail. The broad quarters make her stiff in strong winds and she makes a delightful, practical dayboat.

## 124 Provident

The ex-Brixham smack *Provident* was built by Sanders and Co., Galmpton, Devon, in 1924, during the flush of Brixham's fishing revival after 1918. She is said to be named for an earlier smack sunk in 1917, as were many of the Brixham and Plymouth sailing trawlers.

*Provident*'s dimensions of 70ft 5in overall, 60ft waterline length, 18ft beam and 9ft 6in draught are typical of these trawling ketches, which, if under about 40 tons, were known as 'Mules' at Brixham. Larger smacks were sometimes referred to as 'the big sloops' after the rig of the original Brixham smacks.

In 1951 the *Provident* was acquired by the Island Cruising Club, based at Salcombe, but is now owned by the Maritime Trust and is leased to the club.

In this photograph her skipper has, for some reason, decided to sail with the jib headed topsail set above a two-reefed mainsail, yet she carries a big foresail and a yard topsail on the mizzen.

The main topsail is set on a wire 'leader' or backstay to tauten the luff. The rounded shape of the lower strake of bulwark planking was a feature of their construction.

These smacks liked wind, and 'a reef and topsail breeze' was desirable for trawling, with a single reef in mainsail and mizzen and a main topsail set above. Brixham smacks used reef lacings instead of points to save chafe. The bobstay and bowsprit shrouds are additions for yacht use, as traditionally the Brixham smacks did not have them.

*Provident*'s bold sheer ends in a square counter but some later smacks, such as the *Vigilance*, had an elliptical stern.

107

### 125 Heloise

The cutter *Heloise* was built in 1900 at Millom, Cumberland, on the Solway Firth, as a fishing craft for trawling prawns, shrimps or flat fish. Like many similar cutters she was converted to a yacht, in 1905, and was sailed to the east coast by new owners in 1912, remaining there until 1926.

After ownership in the Channel Islands and on the south coast, the *Heloise* was bought by Mr and Mrs Brian Langsley in 1972 who, with enthusiasm typical of owners of such craft, partially reconstructed the hull and re-rigged her.

When in fishing trim these cutters set a very long gaff with a low angle of peak, and the sail plan usually needed a long bowsprit and large jib to balance. The hulls were mostly built from lines lifted from a scale half model made by the builder, sometimes a solid, carved model or often sections with ribbands (battens) bent around them to achieve the desired shape. Draught was light for the boats intended for prawning and shrimping the shallow gutways amongst the sands, when a crew of up to four might be working a boat, and catches of prawns and shrimps were boiled in a copper in the large well.

Other cutters of the north-west coast which fished mainly the channels, were of deeper draught

These boats worked on an exposed coast with strong tides, where a trawling breeze raised a steep, breaking sea. Early boats had plumb stems, a long straight keel, sloop rig and a transom stern.

After about 1895 the builders evolved craft which had features from current yacht practice, the forefoot being well rounded and cut-away, bow sections were fined, sternpost rake increased and the keel profile rounded as external ballast began to be fitted. This improved type was fully developed by about 1903 and fished from many places from Annan in the north to Aberystwyth, Wales, in the south, and varied in length from about 30 to 48 feet and widely in hull form as these north-west builders were fond of experiment.

### 127 Sall

The 24 ft 2 in *Sall* is one of a range of small traditional cutters designed by John Leather. She was built at Maldon, Essex, by Walter Cook and Son in 1967 and has cruised to Belgium, Holland, Germany, Denmark, Sweden and Finland under David Grose, her present owner, who sails from the Beaulieu River, Hampshire.

The clinker-planked *Sall* is 22 ft 1 in waterline length, 8 ft 6 in beam and 3 ft 6 in draught. She sets 377 square feet and has a 10 h.p. diesel auxiliary. Two or four berths, a galley and toilet are worked in, with roomy, flush decks. New craft like this carry the traditions of gaff rig into modern use.

## 26 Moya

The *Moya*'s sun-hatted and guernseyed crew bring
a touch of past style to a gaff rig race, compli-
menting the smartness of her pale and dark green
sides and tan terylene sails.

She was built in 1910 by Crossfield Brothers at
Arnside as a yacht, reputedly to lines lifted from
a half model, then still a common method of form

design on that coast.

Hull dimensions are 42 ft 6 in overall length,
35 ft waterline, 11 ft 7 in beam and 6 ft 6 in draught.
Launched as a cutter, she was later converted to
yawl rig and is now restored to a fine example of
a gaff cutter, with eyelets for a balance reef in the
mainsail, for use in bad weather. The guard rails,
winch on the boom, and the permanent boom

gallows are modern additions.

Roger Smith's photograph shows the sleek lines
of her hull, derived from the many similar sized
trawling smacks constructed by Crossfield's, who
also produced several other yachts. The rounded,
shallow counter is typical, as is the modest freeboard. They are usually fast to windward in
moderate conditions but can be wet in a seaway.

## 128 Wild Goose

The chine hulled *Wild Goose* had been slipping along splendidly when things went wrong with her gaff jaws. Roger Smith chose that moment to photograph Mr Gifford's boat and it illustrates what can happen with yard topsails in the best regulated yachts.

## 129 Pierce Eye

*Pierce Eye* is a Walton and Frinton Yacht Club one-design still sailing with a gunter mainsail and therefore technically ineligible for inclusion in a book on gaff rig craft. However, she is a good example of what can be done in preservation and has a useful cuddy top added on the forward end of the cockpit.

This able class of centreboard racers was designed by Morgan Giles and they were built by Brooke and Halls at Walton-on-Naze between 1921-23. They raced as a class until the 1950s. Dimensions are 18 ft overall length, 16 ft 9 in waterline length, beam 5 ft 9 in and sail area is 220 square feet. They cost £140 new in 1921.

**130 A small gaff-rigged boat**

Besides being the most cheerful photograph in this book, perhaps this little boat best expresses the spirit of the revival of gaff rig by sailing people willing to fit-out even the smallest craft to get afloat.

She is about 14 ft long, a centreboarder, usually rigged as a sloop with the foresail on a short bowsprit, but can become a cutter by simply rigging a light bamboo bowsprit and jib. The almost horizontal gaff mars the appearance of this handy rig but allows a long luff with a short mast, which is well stayed with a pair of shrouds on each side.

This is a good example of what can be done with a superannuated one-design hull. There are many such sailing dinghies having good beam and stability, lying in odd corners of watersides, out of favour in a dinghy racing world demanding plastic or cold-moulded hulls, aluminium spars, extreme speed and wet suited crews. Often well built old boats can be acquired for modest amounts out of all proportion to the enjoyment they can give.